Holiday in Hell

Holiday In Hell

by

TRISHA SMITH

ASTEROID
PUBLISHING

Asteroid Publishing, Inc.

Please contact Asteroid Publishing, Inc.
P.O. Box 3, Richmond Hill, ON. Canada L4C 4X9

editor@asteroidpublishing.ca

www.asteroidpublishing.ca

ISBN: 978-0-9731379-6-5

Author photograph taken by Keyhan.

ATTENTION ORGANIZATIONS, SCHOOLS AND HUMAN RIGHTS INSTITUTIONS: Quantity discounts are available on bulk purchases of this book.

Moved by being unable to charge her perpetrator of a brutal crime against her, a woman seeks an amendment to the Canadian *Criminal Code 6(2)*. She reveals in her story her darkest moments, and some surprising twist of coincidences, which enable her to persevere in her quest for justice.

Because sentence against evil work is not executed speedily, therefore the heart of the sons of men is fully set in them to do evil.

Ecclesiastes 8:11

My gratitude could never cease...
To my family, even my two grandsons, who have been
supportive and throughout this time have had faith
that sooner or later justice will prevail!

To those who are my lifetime friends and those who became
participants in the journey to bring this book to reality.
Many Thanks!

Table of Contents

PROLOGUE

I'm awakened by the familiar screeching sound of rubber on tarmac. Instead of arriving home from a tropical holiday with a refreshed body, mind, and spirit, this time the sound irritates me and fills me with overwhelming anxiety.

Cathy touches my arm.

"Marisha, we're home," she whispers into my ear.

I'm the first to deplane. Standing up, pain cascades from my face to my toes. Painstakingly, I hold onto each seat I pass. Slowly, I move with my head bowed toward the stewardess walking ahead of me. Each passenger's stare burns through my wounded face. I'm dazed and unable to see clearly through my unbandaged swollen eye. Cathy reminds me of what I must do officially.

"As soon as the captain hands him over to the police," she reminds me, "you must point at him and speak as loudly as you can that you charge this man with assaulting you in Cuba."

I gasp for air, desperate to get out of the aircraft to the place where I see a wheelchair. It is there; the stewardess helps me to ease myself down into it. Cathy and Randolph are still beside me, standing on each side. The stewardess requests them to leave with the remaining passengers. I ache with their parting from me. These two have become caring friends, even though they are only acquaintances who exchanged vacationers' stories with me on the island. I beg them to stay; I want to keep their comfort around me. But the stewardess quickly pushes me in the opposite direction, down the ramp to another arrival hall, a darker one, and leaves.

I breathe a sigh of relief. There in a corner under what looks like a blue-white spotlight, I see him surrounded. I hope that the Canadian authorities already have arrested him.

I raise my trembling hand and wave in his direction.

"I charge Raffaele Grecci for assaulting me in Cuba! I charge him now in Canada!"

A deathly silence fills the hallway.

"You cannot charge this man in Canada for an assault in Cuba," one of the many officers replies.

I can't believe what I'm hearing. I'm devastated! In this gut-wrenching moment, everything freezes.

"I . . . I . . . I can't charge him?" I yell.

"No," another police officer adds.

My heart palpitates; my breathing stops as I lift myself up a few agonizing inches off the wheelchair seat. The policewoman eases me back and hands me a Kleenex.

I wipe my bleeding nose and feel a prickle of pain in my mouth, especially now, when I yell.

"He attacked me! He almost killed me!"

I crumple back down into the wheelchair seat and feel myself beginning to black out as I see the man who had savagely beaten me swagger away. It's as though prison bars are closing on me, instead of him.

What on earth is happening in my homeland? I carried out the instructions of the Cuban police!

"I–I–I was promised! H–h–he was going to be a–a–rrested!" I stutter.

No answer.

Anger and fear turn to panic; I can barely clear my throat. Am I not the victim?

"Why? Why? Why?" I yell.

"Sorry, we have no jurisdiction to act on a crime that occurred in Cuba," another officer states.

"What do you mean, there's no jurisdiction? He's a Canadian citizen and so am I! This is ridiculous!"

"Why can't you understand?" The older officer frowns. "There's no law in Canada to charge him for a crime committed in Cuba."

I'm trembling, devastated and stunned in disbelief.

"I–I–I need protection," I stutter again, glaring at the silent wall of blue uniforms standing in front of me. It appears that he has gotten away scot-free, immune from punishment. With my last ounce of effort, I cry out, again, "I've been—brutally—attacked! Can't you see?! He almost killed me!!"

"I'm truly sorry," the policewoman responds with almost genuine compassion, "but we don't have the authority."

My trepidation makes my heart pound so hard; I fear I'm on the verge of having a coronary. She hands me another Kleenex. I wipe my tears and blot my nose, the tissue revealing the warm red liquid that is still flowing.

"Can you please take me to the hospital?" I beg.

Instead, she wheels me out to the passenger pickup area.

"Are you taking me to the hospital?"

I feel frustrated, overcome by fatigue.

"Sorry, we cannot do that," she answers. She points to a phone at the courtesy desk and then stomps away, shaking her head.

I'm alone—confused, embarrassed, and abandoned.

I wonder who to call.

I curse the day I met him.

Chapter I. Charming First Meeting

My psychologist in her navy suit comes across relaxed; she speaks in a quiet and soothing tone.

"To heal this terrible mental trauma, we have to understand how and why it occurred." Her soft voice calms me a bit. She leans forward to continue. "I may ask you questions, some of which may seemingly not be related to the issue. You are welcome to interrupt me anytime for any explanation, discussion, or whatever."

Her dark eyes and arched brow convey genuine compassion; the quiet ambience of her warmly decorated office is conducive to our frank discussion. I nod in agreement.

"You are a teacher, Marisha, aren't you?"

"Yes, I am."

"Do you like your profession?"

I pause, observing a photograph of her with her family.

"Passionately. I'm an artist, too. Teaching was a career change, but I do it, as everything else, with passion and love."

"You must be a very successful teacher then? Am I right?"

"That's how I think of myself. It's important for me to enjoy my work," I explain, and then add, "What I have just recounted to you makes me want to explode."

She nods, showing an understanding of my feelings. I continue.

"Am I going to regain my good life back?"

"In a sense. You see," the psychologist folds her palms, "as a teacher, you meet a lot of different people, kids and adults. A successful teacher quickly finds the right approach to all sorts of individuals, understands their abilities—the whole gamut of their idiosyncrasies."

"True, but what does this has to do with . . . ?" I ask. It does not make any sense to me how I could have been assaulted like this—not only by the attacker, but even more so, by the Canadian justice system.

"I'm getting to that, Marisha. I want to understand how this happened to you, the person with such good insight into human nature. Didn't you recognize in your former boyfriend his violent disposition? Was there any hint?"

"No. He treated me with respect."

"If it isn't too painful for you, can you tell me, at least briefly, how your romance—if we can call it that—commenced?"

My inner vision rolls in succession, like a movie, all scenes and images having crisp clarity. But because of my blurred memory, affected by the horrific assault, I couldn't grasp exactly whether I was silently watching this movie or whether I was conveying the story to the psychologist sitting in her armchair across from me.

It was during the summer of 1998. I was meeting my friends for a bit of a celebration. *Hemingway's* in Yorkville at that time has survived the fickleness of changing trends over the past few decades. The multilevel, bustling neighbourhood pub was sandwiched between the Four Seasons Hotel on one side and an array of nouveaux chic boutiques on the other. All had transformed Cumberland Street into Rodeo Drive North.

Next to a large, open window overlooking the crowded patio, I'm seated with four other friends at the perfect table. Normally, we meet here and then move to *Movenpick* or *Sassafraz* for dinner; it's our favourite spot. This time of year, the terraces are especially full of tourists, so we opt to keep this comfortable setting, for now. As it is, we are already indulging in our favourite pastime—people-watching and sipping wine.

Good friends, good conversation, and a great venue. Everyone is bubbling with laughter. Summer is soon approaching, and for us it's holiday time!

Monica is married to a wonderful, hardworking businessman. Both of them are blonds, fairer than most Northern Italians. Sometimes, Monica and I are mistaken for sisters. It's our blue eyes; her Italian appearance is more like my Slavic look. Monica's marriage produced three healthy, beautiful—and now grown—children. I had met her in college when we both were slowly but surely working toward our degree on a part-time basis. Through the university work, we had become professional colleagues.

This evening must now be the third end-of-the-school-year celebration that we have enjoyed so far together. Dana, on the other side of the table is also in her late thirties. Her dark, Romanian, slightly slanted brown eyes and skin contrast with her short-trimmed blond locks. I have met her only recently through attending a spiritual conference. During breaks, we would talk about being single, good dining, dancing, and relationships. Now Dana and I do more than talk on the telephone; we meet with our friends, just as we're doing now. Dana's close friend Samantha is sitting beside me, across from Dana. Sam, as Dana calls her, has a melodic accent with a distinguished South American look. Her education is in international business law, and she now has a great job at Canadian Tourism. Her downtown office is just around the corner, just as is my friend Ruth's. This is what made it convenient for us to meet here. Ruth—well, I call her "Ruthie" most of the time—works on King Street. Sometimes she's forced to work late. This is why she has just arrived and sat down beside Dana, across from me. Her shining dark eyes piercing through her curly hair and especially her laughter bring joy to our group. Everyone greets each other; our table tallies five.

Everyone is speaking at the same time, eager to share plans for the summer. Monica is off to Europe with her husband. Dana will be teaching in Rome. Ruth is longing for weekends in Muskokas. Samantha has Montreal and the Grand Prix at the top of her activities list. What a wonderful life!

Me, I don't care, I'm glad not to have any. The world is coming to me. I have two exchange students, one from Osaka and another from Hong Kong.

Dinner draws to a close on a common note—summer was long overdue.

We exit *Hemingway's* as twilight slowly yields tonight. Outside, the imitation gas lanterns in black iron seem to light up instantly.

"We're already late!" Samantha announces.

The temptation to include window-shopping today is out of the question. Instead, we take the shortcut on the old stone alleyway, which crosses both streets of Cumberland and Yorkville. We navigate slowly through a gauntlet of street buskers on our way to join other friends, who are awaiting us at *Club Centra*.

From a half-block away, we spot the six-foot three-inch Michael, who's towering over Crystal, waving to us. They're both dressed in all-white loose clothing and Brian, as usual, is outfitted in a standard charcoal Versace suit. We wave back and agree to quicken our pace.

Michael's brown wavy hair is longer now; his dark skin is shining, and he's heavier than I remember him being. He greets us with Crystal by his side; she has become part of his everyday life. When we do our usual hug, it's Michael and Crystal squeezing each other and sandwiching me. Then there's Brian, who's a bit shy; his type of hello is a short wave of his hand and a bright smile.

Our greetings are interrupted; Michael is introducing to us an unfamiliar face.

"Everyone, this is Ralph. Ralph, this is everyone."

Jeff, the enormously muscled doorman, smiles, lifts the burgundy rope and signals Brian, as we pass the long line-up. The heavy iron and glass doors open; another bouncer steers us to a table close to the dance floor. Before we sit down, Ruth whispers over the music,

"What do you think of him?"

"Who?" I respond, knowing exactly who she's talking about.

"You know," she says and then energetically touches my arm.

I smile with approval, seeing that he's also eyeing me from across the table.

"Marisha, he can't take his eyes off you," Ruth whispers and then giggles.

I'm taken by his magnificent dark eyes. I'm mesmerized, no doubt. But I don't want to be obvious about it. I ask Ruth,

"Let's go get some sushi."

Each Friday night, *Club Centra* offers sushi—it's a treat I can't resist. I spot him still looking at me. I guess we are both attracted.

"Look, Marisha! He's a really good-looking guy."

"Stop it, Ruthie." I laughingly respond to her teasing me, as my eyes still focus in his way—observing that he's dressed immaculately in a nice green suit with an open-collar polo shirt. Then, I look away toward the swaying bodies on the dance floor as the DJ spins a mixed of reggae, Euro, and now salsa; Ralph follows my every move and smiles at me. Michael and Crystal are busy dancing away. Dana and Monica are talking to some people who just sat down beside them, and Brian is chatting with Ralph. Ralph is still looking at me.

Ruth and I continue eating sushi, spin occasionally on the barstools toward the crowd, and chat about her weekends up north; I'm thinking about him. Every time I meet his eyes, he's still smiling. Ruth gently touches my hand, as if she's trying to wake me from a trance.

"Come on Marisha, Dana and Sam want to dance" Ruth calls joyfully. Dana smiles and nods; then Samantha, a huge smile on her beautiful Peruvian face, gets up as we approach them and says to me, "Let's strut our Latino stuff!"

Everyone joins Michael and Crystal on the dance floor, including the people with whom Dana and Sam were talking, and without exception Ralph and Brian are here dancing beside me. More kaleidoscope strobe lights rhythmically pulsate to the music around us.

In the glare of the lights, his curly dark hair and face appear even more handsome, right now as he dancers toward me. His lips pour out some words amidst the heavy bass lines; the music drowns out any chance to start a decent conversation. Samantha, Dana, and Ruth retreat to our spot. I follow them, sensing that Ralph is not far behind me. He stops beside my chair and leans down.

"Can I sit here, next to you?"

He speaks with an air of confidence, but not conceit. I nod, "Sure," and smile,

"Would you ladies like a drink?" he asks and quickly gestures toward the waiter passing by.

Across the table, Ruth and Michael beam with the air of successful matchmakers. The waiter returns with drinks.

11

"Cheers!" I offer Ralph a smile.

"Cheers!" everyone replies.

"Wouldn't it be great to try it out?" he turns to me and asks when the conversation around the table is about some salsa dance classes held here at *Club Centra*. I don't get a chance to respond. Everyone already agrees, "Sounds like it would be fun."

"Boy, is it ever hot in here," Ralph says, wiping a few beads of sweat from his forehead.

"Maybe the air-conditioning isn't working," Ruth says as she comes to sit beside me; I nod.

"Let's go to the restroom, Marisha," she whispers, and we excuse ourselves, leaving Ralph alone at the table. Everyone is doing their own thing, except for Michael and Crystal, who are chatting on a circular sofa, beside the open windows.

Two steps inside the washroom, Ruth turns to me.

"So what do you think of him? He seems nice, Marisha."

Raising an eyebrow, she nudges me, again. "Well, what do you think?"

"He seems very nice," I smile and add, "It's hard to tell until I have a chance to get to know him."

After a quick check in the mirror, we leave the washroom. We return to our table. Ralph stands up quickly and brushes his hair back with both hands. This time, one hand supports my back and the other points to the seat next to him.

"I've kept this seat for you." He lets out another smile.

I slide down beside him. Samantha, Ruth, and Monica are now sitting on the other side. Monica strikes up a conversation. Without hesitation, Ralph leans toward her and tells a joke. Everyone reels with laughter. Michael and Crystal now join us and fan themselves with the cocktail menus. "It's so stifling in here." I fan myself with my hand. "Is anyone up for moving to the patio?" Michael, holding Crystal close, suggests.

On the terrace, the night's cool breeze relieves the summer's humid stickiness. Jokes and one-liners continue to fly between us. Ralph edges closer to me. Without a doubt, I conclude that he's definitely going to ask me for a real date.

We return to dance for few more songs, and then Ralph asks, "Would you please call me?" He hands me his business card. I can smell his Giorgio Armani cologne. He seems to be a true gentleman.

My psychologist sighs, returning me to the reality of her small office—my physical and emotional anguish overrides any good memory of him or any joy of ever having known him.

"You asked me if there was any indication of his violent character. I'm struggling for an answer. I hope to address this at our next session, if you don't mind."

Chapter 2. Documenting Pain

Painful and boring matters are priorities in my life, with no time for anything else. Otherwise, anxiety sets in all the more. My health is fragile; I have to see my family doctor, very soon.

In a room full of patients, the welcoming smile on my doctor's face vanishes. I'm relieved that he's speechless and quickly gestures for me to come into the examination room.

He peels off the bandages and notes my injuries: the heavy bruising on my face, neck, and arms; the swelling throughout my upper torso; the scratches, abrasions, and deep cut under my right eye; my fractured nose; and the bite mark on my right shoulder. He records them silently on his clipboard and calls for his assistant to bring a camera. He's more concerned about the cut under my right eye, right now.

"It's infected," he says. "We need to get rid of the infection before I can take any of the stitches out." He dabs some cream under my eyes. "Apply the antibiotic cream a few times a day. The bruising will mend; however, for the broken nose you'll have to see a specialist. I'll order an MRI for your spine."

This kind of prognosis is not what I want to hear, but I am thankful for the doctor's thoroughness.

"Ask your dentist to take X-rays of your teeth. In the long run, who knows how these injuries could affect your gums and then your teeth."

"Morty, my head is pounding. And, for the last few days, I've been more on the toilet than off."

"Keep drinking your herbal remedies and the green tea," he says, as he knows my healthy ways, and then adds, "Perhaps you can tell me briefly what happened? If, of course, it's not too . . ."

"It's okay, doctor. It happened in Cuba, where I was on trip—a holiday in hell."

I don't remember exactly how I told him the story, but I vividly remember every bit of the trauma.

It is the last night in the resort. Ralph has just brought me back to my room, after an embarrassing conversation with other vacationers. Once we enter the suite, I say,

"I need some sleep. It's only a few hours until we leave for the airport."

I lie down, watching a brilliant moonbeam flickering through the sheer curtains. I'm mesmerized by the bright reflection dancing on my tanned legs and pearl-coloured toenails. Ralph is having his last cigarette out on the balcony. I call to him to rest and watch the moonlight's glow with me, as I'm already falling into a deep sleep.

Before long, I wake up in terror, gasping for air and screaming uncontrollably. I'm in pain, horrified, yelling for help. Shocked! I see dark stains on the sheets; it's my own blood, dripping.

"No! No! Stop it!" I scream, waking up.

The moonlight casting its bright light through the tall balcony window allows me to see my own blood gushing into the sheets and pillows. I hope to free myself from the grip of my attacker, but one of his hands holds me down, the other pounds my face.

"I'll kill you! I'll kill you!" he yells, over again and again.

I flail my arms and twist my head to get free, but I'm yanked back on the bed, my head swinging back and forth with the impact of each blow.

"God help me! God help me! Let me go!"

Like a mad animal, my attacker keeps pummelling me. With each blow to my face and head, he becomes more violent.

"Please let me go, please let me go!" I'm trying to get my breath. The feel of the blood gets thicker and thicker. I can't see.

"Why? Why, are you doing this? Please let me go!" I gasp.

He does not stop hitting me. My face streams with blood. My vision blurs—I start losing consciousness, but inside I'm screaming for my life.

"Let me go!!!"

Despair and fear of imminent death give me one last ounce of strength. I free myself, finally, and slide off the bed onto all fours on the hard floor, then quickly push myself to crawl toward the exit, grabbing a robe lying nearby. I slide across the marble floor made slippery by my blood.

He is getting closer. "Now, I'm going to jail for sure." His voice terrifies me: I know it like I know my own.

"Help me! Someone, please help me!" Screaming, I manage to get outside. Confronted, now, by the stairs, I'm afraid of falling down—afraid of dying on display, stretched out in a bloody puddle. I don't want to die like this. I don't know how I half run, half stagger, scrambling down the stairs. Somehow, I reach the bottom, careening against the walls like a wounded animal running for its life. Behind me, his footsteps get louder, like a threatening drumbeat. My fingers scrape on the walls, groping for a door. "Someone, help me! Help me! Help me! Help me! Please someone, help!"

Beads of perspiration stand on my face, as the doctor says, "Take it easy!" I cough, and stop talking. The doctor nods.

"I'm going to prescribe Paxil."

"What's that?" I stutter and cough, trying to clear my throat.

"It's a mild antidepressant to ease your anxiety. I'm also prescribing Ciprofloxacin, a painkiller, and Relafen, an anti-inflammatory. Make sure you follow the instructions. And, if the infection under the eye is still there tomorrow, please call my office."

The prescriptions go into my purse; I'm upset that I have to take all this medication. Halfway out the door, I remember that I still have a profession.

"Oh, doctor, could you please write me a sick-leave notice for the school board?"

"Certainly," he says, pauses, and then further advises me. "You know that for your protection, you must get a restraining order against him, immediately. You'll not heal over night, and the last thing you need is for that idiot to be anywhere near you. Don't forget to call the crisis unit at York Central, and I suggest that you also contact the Yellow Brick House for counseling. They assist with trauma counseling and legal matters."

I watch my doctor write the information down for me.

"Their head office is in Aurora, but they have a location nearby, on Yonge Street. Julia, the counselor, is excellent."

He hands me his paperwork and reminds me, "You need to see me once a week, and come back in a few days to have the stitches removed."

I hate going out in public—the exposure embarrasses me; I can't handle the constant "what happened to you?" let alone the staring.

"See you, in a few days, for those stitches."

Back at home, I collapse on the bed, exhausted by pain and humiliated by everyone's attention to my face. The newly prescribed mixture of medication and my own natural remedies upset my stomach. I feel like I'm going to blow up.

More than that, the question of my psychologist haunts me whenever I am alone. I analyze each day of that relationship: Was there any sign? What did I miss? Even now, as much as I hate and despise this man, I admit that our romance was beautiful from the very first day I met him. That day was at the end of grading exams for another school year.

I reflect on that Saturday night: Should I call him? The weekend is almost here. Why not? I dial the number from his business card, only to hear the familiar voice on the answering machine. Perhaps I should leave him my phone number? No. I'd rather get him later.

About an hour later I redial. This time, when the machine comes on, I leave a message, "Hi Ralph. It's Marisha. We met last Saturday. Here's my phone number. . . . Call me when you have a chance."

"Mom, are you ready?" Katrina, my daughter, eager for our shopping venture, hollers from her room upstairs as the phone rings. It's Ralph, for sure. I run to the kitchen. My intuition serves me well.

"I'm fine," I say to him while trying to control my excitement.

"I was worried that you'd never call," he lets me know, and waits.

"Well, here I am, Ralph."

"Are you free this weekend?"

"I still have some exams to correct."

"When would you be finished?"

"Actually, tonight is good for me."

"Well, how about dinner?"

"That sounds nice."

"What time?"

"I'm just on my way out the door to go shopping with my daughter." I put Ralph on hold because Katrina is calling in the background.

"Mom, are you ready?"

"Sure, honey. I'm waiting for you downstairs."

I get back to Ralph, and we arrange the date.

"So, seven o'clock?" he asks.

"Sure, Ralph."

"Great. Should I pick you up at your home or should we meet somewhere?"

"How about somewhere in Yorkville?"

He suggests *Mabella's* patio.

"All right! Then I'll see you at *Mabella's*, sevenish," I reply.

"Hey, mom! Is this a date tonight?" Katrina asks from the hallway.

"How could you tell?"

"Look at you! You're smiling like a Cheshire cat."

We laugh as we head out to the car.

"So, what's up with your big date, Mom?"

"Did I mention Ralph? I met him last Saturday. This evening, he's invited me to dinner."

"Nice!"

"It's just a dinner date, Katrina." She smiles lovingly. I continue, "We'll see. So, what are you up to this evening?"

"Dan and I are going with a few friends to see a movie."

"Looks like for a change we'll both be out tonight!" I nudge Katrina with my elbow.

This time our shopping is done in record time.

"Mom, get ready! It's already 6:15," Katrina encourages me.

"Thanks, Katrina!" I give her a quick peck on the cheek, "You're wonderful!"

Then I disappear to my room upstairs. The radio plays another top-twenty hit. My image in the mirror moves to the rhythm as I brush my hair, crack a smile of approval, and head down the stairs.

"Katrina, I'm r-e-a-d-y!"

In harmony with the world, if not the song, in the car I sing at the top of my lungs, "It's a beau-ti-ful day."

It's not hard to pick Ralph out of the swarm at *Mabella's*: He's waiting for me, leaning against the entrance. His hair glistens; his face is very handsome. He sees me, straightens himself up quickly, and walks toward me, his eyes on me. Now face-to-face, I like how he takes my hand in his and kisses it, gently squeezing it.

"Hey, Marisha, you look great."

"Thank you." I want to return the compliment, but decide to do it later.

He leads me to the table at the far end of the patio. Two white chairs are sitting across from each other; he has obviously reserved it. He asks me to sit across from him, where I look away from the crowd, facing only him.

"Would you like something to drink?" he asks and gestures to the headwaiter.

I notice his voice is hoarse, not the same as last Saturday. I think, perhaps, he smokes cigarettes. I'll find out later. He looks good tonight; not only is his sense of style put together just right, but he also has a new, styled haircut.

"I'm happy that we were able to meet today," he says. I nod.

21

"I hope you don't mind ordering dinner a bit later?" Ralph suggests, and then continues, "Well, here we are!" He cheers with the glass of sparking water, smiles, and smoothes his hair. I give him a nod of approval. "You look very handsome, Ralph!"

He smiles easily and assures me, "I'm glad to see you again, Marisha."

I'm becoming used to him taking my hand in his and kissing it as he looks into my eyes.

"I'm privileged to have you sitting here with me," he continues, and caresses my hand.

I feel a bit overwhelmed by his actions and words. Such a romantic beginning! The only thing I can think of to say to him is, "You're so sweet! Thank you."

He talks about himself: his business, where his office is, where he lives, and other things so necessary to know for developing trust and understanding.

"How long have you lived in that area?" I ask.

"Well." He stops, and I can see a faint flush come over his cheeks. He finally responds, "I live with my parents for now." He pauses again, then resumes, "Well, until I find a place of my own."

"So, you moved back in with your parents?"

Seemingly irritated by my question, he reveals, "After my divorce . . ." He pauses. "Well, I was forced to." He clears his throat.

"Aha." I try to help him with a meaningless exclamation.

Our conversation feels overburdened with Ralph's life—I hear the sounds of the alto cello strings playing harshly over the newfound sweet romantic violins. I want to keep the talk light, and quickly change the topic. I ask him if his work involves traveling outside the country. "Most of my business is done in the office, making long-distance calls. However, I love to travel, for pleasure." Nonchalantly he continues to mention scenes from some of his favorite tropical places. His last exotic destination had been just a few months ago, a holiday in Mexico.

I've trekked quite a bit on foreign soil myself, so I share with him my previous experiences living and traveling in different countries. He says how he visits his parents' vacation place in Europe and loves reconnecting with family there. Then I tell him, jokingly, how I managed to survive in Italy by flipping quickly through *A Rough Guide to Italian*.

I detect a surge of positive energy between Ralph and me. Trust is building and our sharing seems to be more comfortable now.

He appears pleasantly shocked when I tell him that my younger daughter, Katrina, is 17 and my older daughter, Daniella, is 21, living in England.

"Marisha, I can't believe you have girls that old!"

"Thank you. I'm blessed," I reply.

We both laugh a bit and take another sip of our drinks. "Cheers!" Then he takes out a pack of cigarettes and lights one. I guess he occasionally smokes. I presume this is why his voice was so hoarse when I first arrived.

Trusting never comes easy, especially when there has been a previous marriage, a broken heart, an awful separation, not to mention the ordeals of a divorce. But as we exchange stories, we continue to give each other permission to find out more about the other.

23

"Tell me, Marisha, how long have you lived in Toronto?"

"Over ten years, now."

"You mean you never remarried? That's nearly impossible."

He knows now that I have been divorced for years. I blush and change the subject, quickly asking him how long he has been separated.

"I've been divorced for two years, now," he says, then pauses and adds, "The only woman in my life now is my daughter, Anna."

"How old is Anna?"

"She's just four," he says. I enjoy listening to the stories he tells me about how he adores her and how sweet she is. "She's my little princess!"

This is what I would usually say about my two daughters; Ralph has the same love for his offspring as I do for mine. Character reveals itself through interaction with children. A man who adores his daughter is a good man. It took a bit of time for me to discover how wrong my perception was!

I think that when I get a chance to interact with Anna and Ralph, I will really know him. He continues, "She's the joy of my life!" I agree with him since my children are exactly that in my life.

"It's definitely a legacy to bring them up in God's ways so that they will have good character!" I say.

The evening gives way to night as our conversation deepens. Our faces, lit by the antique street lanterns, create a romantic moment.

Time passes more quickly than I can remember for months, even years.

"I guess it's time to leave!" Ralph announces. We both laugh. "How about that!" He says, pauses, then adds, "We have outlasted everyone!"

As we head down the pebbled sidewalk, we pass some of the usual Yorkvilleites: a palm reader, a flamingo musician, and a panhandler. Then, a Charlie Chaplin look-alike appears, cradling a huge bunch of roses as if they were his babies. With a gesture, he hands me a rose-coloured one, and of course he's smiling at Ralph, whose hand is bouncing some change to get it out of his pocket and places the coins into the man's large palm.

He smiles and tells me, "This has been a memorable evening for me. You're such a lovely lady and I want to see more of you!"

The affection is mutual, but I place the keys into the car door. He opens it for me.

"When can I see you again, Marisha?"

"I'm just a phone call away, Ralph."

Knowing that we like each other enough, there's no need to schedule the next date. I crank the ignition; he straightens himself and closes the door of my car. As he walks to his jeep, he says, "I'll call you!"

I wave back, thinking, "What a great guy!"

***

Necessities are the only activities in or out of my house. My aging mother enters the room, as does my dog, Bito, yanking me back to the hell of reality. Mother shops, cooks, and feeds me. I hate to feel like a child, again. Bito

25

follows me through the house; he does not even demand to be walked.

My right cheekbone, jaw, and gums are very tender; I cannot chew, so Mom purees my food. She swabs my wounds with ointments given to her by a friend. I see her eyes saddened; she looks upon my beaten and broken state, with dread.

My mother walks Bito and documents my injuries with a disposable camera—a macabre Kodak moment. She takes the two rolls of film for one-hour development. Then she places them in a grim album to preserve the evidence of a vicious crime perpetrated on her only daughter.

I don't know how many days I fall in and out of sleep, often waking in a cold sweat. I hear the words, "I'll kill you! I'll kill you!" I tear the elastic from my hair and scream, "Let me go! Let me go!" I hear my mother at my bedroom door: "Marisha! You're at home! You're safe!"

She hands me some water and another two tablets to ease my pain; then, she gives me a warm wet cloth to wipe the blood that still trickles from my mouth. Bito, confused by my behaviour, moans almost nonstop.

Again, I wake up, not knowing what day it is, let alone what time.

My mother has made cabbage soup—her special "medicine"—and she implores me to come downstairs to eat. I can barely hobble, but I know moving around will probably help me. She sits across the table from me and coaxes me to eat, then watches intensely as I begin to say grace; her only response is to make the sign of the cross.

As I take a careful sip of broth, my mother tells me that Monica called while I slept. I ask her if Monica wants me to call her back. She tells me that Monica is concerned whether I have received the Cuban declaration papers and says that it will probably be necessary to get a restraining order against Ralph. I'm grateful for friends like her.

I look at the meticulously organized folder, which mother places before me. She has organized all the medical documents from the hospitals, along with the papers she has found in my luggage and purse. This type of task was once a part of her life working as a nurse during World War II.

I pull the dark binder with the portable phone on top of it toward me and think about calling Cuba. I open the folder and flip through the results of 48 hours of having been poked, prodded, assessed, and insulted. Then I come across an informative pamphlet from the hospital.

"Mom, you won't believe what I'm reading. Look at this absurdity. The hospital has tested me for an 'Animal Bite.' Can you believe this?"

"He's truly an animal," my mom cries out. "Marisha, in the old country we immediately shot dogs that bite."

"Check this out Mom," I say to my mom. "'Reported animal bites (wild or domestic) are investigated by Public Health. The patient should notify Public Health or the Police Department, who will try to locate the animal so that it may be assessed and observed for disease risk.'"

We both share an almost forced, yet welcomed smile.

Chapter 3. Terrifying Evidence

For days, I wake up in the middle of the night, sweating and trembling, scared out of my wits by a nightmare. However, being awake is not better; my merciless memory takes me back to the last night in Cuba.

Out of the iron grips and blows of my attacker, dashing down the stairs from him, I vaguely recall that my new acquaintances, Liza, Steve, Anna Maria and Mike, live on the first floor. Furiously, determined to save myself, I bang on each door. In the dark doorway, I hear Liza.

"Oh my God, Steve! Come here, fast!"

Like a guardian angel taking me into her sheltering arms, she wraps me in some soft terry covering. I hear the sound of children's voices.

"It's Marisha! Marisha, what happened, what happened?" the children scream with fear.

"Kids, don't look, turn around," Steve says.

I hear him begging, "Please try to stay calm!" Steve waves his hand in front of my face. "Marisha, look here," he calls.

Short, bright flashes of light hurt my half-closed eyes as the camera clicks one frame after another. Liza walks me into the bathroom. The last flash of light from the camera reflects in the mirror, outlining a picture of me covered in my own blood.

I groan with pain, disbelieving what I see. The water pours out of the tap into the sink below and mixes with the blood streaming from my open wounds.

"Bastard," I say, and collapse unconscious into Liza's arms.

The next time I'm certain that I'm still alive is when I try to open my eyes. I feel disoriented and gasp for air. My body is racked with pain. I can barely open an eye or lift my head.

"Please help me!" I look at Liza.

"Marisha, it's okay, you're safe!" Liza's voice says.

I sense that one eye is covered; I strain to focus through the slit of an opening in the other. My blurred vision permits me, only vaguely, to recognize Liza's face nearby. I hear others in the room; they are mere shadows; only their comforting sounds of relief wash over me. Liza covers my hand gently with hers and reaches me through the shock.

"She needs to take these sedatives, right now," Anna Marie's voice says as a hand brings a pill to my mouth. Anna Marie, usually a woman with a bubbling personality, and her husband Mike, with his sense of humour, are now shocked. "Let's see if you can swallow these with water," she says.

I'm comforted by their care, but the liquid stings my lacerated lips and the inside of my mouth, so I pull away.

"Please try to swallow this," another voice says.

Terrifying pain engulfs me, and I realize that I could have been killed. The shock makes me want to scream, but I can only stutter in agony.

"Why did he do this to me, the bastard!" I want to fall asleep and not feel this horror.

"You're safe, now," Liza's voice says.

"Where is he, now?" I'm beyond fear.

"He's guarded by the police," someone says, but I don't recognize the voice.

"Last night, security took him, and then Steve and Adriel, the manager, took you to two hospitals. Do you remember that?" someone asks.

I have no recollection; I must have been in a coma.

"I c . . .can only re . . .remember Steve's voice c . . . calling out to me." My voice sounds strange and high pitched.

I start to cough. Someone hands me a Kleenex. I wipe my mouth; the white tissue is now soaked in blood. Tears flow, uncontrollably, stinging the cuts on my face. Someone blots my face. Each touch is unbearable.

"You're safe now, Marisha," Steve's voice says. "They were not equipped in the first hospital to take X-rays. You had a concussion. The doctor said you were struck on the head by who knows what."

The fear of dying engulfs me as I hear Steve telling me about last night. He says he rushed out to get help and crashed headlong into Ralph; his blood-covered hands wove around, frantically, as if he disowned them. Ralph ranted and raved, in denial of the attack.

"Everyone is shocked, Marisha." Liza takes my hand.

"You had already passed out when we brought the nurse to care for you," Steve says. I listen carefully so I can learn what went on in the last five hours as Steve continues. "Adriel and I, with the help of two security guards, placed you on a stretcher and into the back of a Suzuki Samuri."

"I told Steve that he should go to the hospital with you because it would be better for you to see a familiar face when you regain consciousness," Liza says.

Steve pauses, seeing that I'm gasping for air, and nods to his wife. At once she hands me some medication. The pills stick to the walls of my dry throat. She hands me a drink. I force myself to swallow the pill and hope it will relieve some of my pain. Steve continues telling me what occurred at the hospital. The doctor immediately instructed him to keep me awake by talking to me because I was bleeding quite a bit and falling deep into a coma. I guess this is why I only remember Steve's voice at the hospital. Perhaps this was a blessing in disguise, to save me from the hospital experience. I have always hated hospitals.

I learn from him that the hospital doctor had been afraid to move my body off the gurney before he took the X-rays; he had been concerned that I might have some broken bones. Steve continues to tell me that the doctor cleaned my wounds and then stitched my cuts.

All of a sudden, Steve stops as Maria, the Alba Tour representative, walks into the room.

"I'm so sorry about what happened, Marisha," she says approaching me.

I'm exasperated and can't speak.

"I'm explaining to Marisha what transpired last night at the hospital," Steve tells Maria.

"The doctor took a lot of X-rays to ensure that there are no broken bones." Maria waves a large envelope in front of me. She then turns to Steve. "Did you tell Marisha that you made a statement to the doctor and police about the incident?"

"Not yet," Steve replies. "I was just about to explain it." Then he turns to me. "The doctor took the statement and then he asked me to notify the police right away."

The door opens and two heavy security guards walk in.

"It's time for Marisha's statement," Liza says.

Steve leaves the room. Cathy, Liza, and Anna Marie help me off the bed, walk me out to a carriage parked beside the cabana, and take me to another section of the resort. I cringe at the thought of being seen like this by the tourists and the resort's staff. Cathy holds me in her arms. Maria opens an umbrella to shade me from the light. Why are they taking me to the police? Can't the police come to the room? Each bump on the road in a horse-drawn cart causes me more pain. Each moment brings more pain and makes me realize that my injuries are severe.

We arrive at a small room filled with smells of cooking. The Cuban police are ready for me. They're already two-finger typing on a very old, black Underwood typewriter. A small Bakelite radio hums in the background. The resort nurse lays me down on a cot as the police take my official statement. Maria translates the police questions and my answers. In this confined space, my head begins to throb. Each click of the typewriter keys brings another shockwave. The nurse wipes the blood from my mouth and encourages me to drink liquids; she keeps telling me to stay alert, but the pain is so excruciating that I can't speak anymore.

A doctor arrives and gives me more sedatives. I'm not sure what medications he's putting into my mouth, and I don't really care. I just want relief. I continue describing the horror of last night's attack. Under oath for what seems like hours, I make a formal declaration to the Cuban officials and charge Raffaele Grecci with assaulting me.

"I charge him for attacking me," I say as my mind battles through my grief, trying to recall whether anyone has actually contacted the Canadian consular officials.

"Has the Embassy been contacted?" I ask.

"Si, Signora," the Cuban officer says, then quickly adds, "Your medical condition requires you return to Canada, immediately." Maria translates.

"What did they say?" In my feeble state, I persist to get an answer.

"They have been contacted, and the Canadian police have also been informed. They will be waiting for him at the airport." Maria keeps translating the Cuban official's response.

I don't feel comfortable leaving Cuba until I'm assured that the authorities will issue an official statement, confirming that I have charged him for the attack. I know for a fact that some laws and customs for Canadians abroad don't apply, and the government of Canada cannot intervene in ongoing legal proceedings in other countries or regions unless requested to do so by local authorities. Such requests are rare. So, I keep asking, desperately, of the local police, "Did you press charges, officially, against Raffaele Grecci in Cuba?"

"Yes, we have," the translator replies.

I ask the Cuban authorities to provide me with a copy of their paperwork before I leave the resort.

"Si, Signora! Claro," they respond, after Maria translates my request.

"When you arrive in Canada, the police in your country will handle the affair."

I take solace in their promise.

Steve and the security guards take me by horse-drawn carriage to another room at the resort. Before Steve leaves, he says that a security officer is protecting the room.

Anna Marie and Cathy walk in. Both assure me that they also gave their statements to the police, who told them that he'd be charged upon arrival in Toronto.

Liza leaves the room to give her statement, while the others take turns caring for me. Like two angels they hover over my body. I'm gasping for air and feeling traumatized as I relive the nightmarish attack.

They try to clean me up as much as they can, but my hair is so terribly matted with dry blood that they call for the resort's hairdresser to help them. Liza returns and they decide to put me into a bath. As they are bathing me, they discover a large bite mark on my neck. After they dress me, Liza calls for her husband, Steve, to come back into the room. He's very upset that the doctor did not note this injury and he, diligently, prepares the evidence as he has done throughout this ordeal.

He documents the bite mark on my neck with photographs and asks each one in the room to sign a witness statement; then, he leaves to present this evidence to the Cuban authorities. God bless his diligence. He knows that I'll need as much evidence as possible to prove the crime perpetrated against me.

"Kyle and Kiera wonder how you're doing," Liza says. "The kids would like to see you before you leave to go to the airport."

I try my best not to cry when the children come to say their goodbyes. They return my backgammon board to me. I try to remember only the wonderful times I had spent with them.

Mike and Anna Marie bring my suitcase. Everyone starts to shake their head with disgust when they see Anna Marie holding a clump of my hair in her hand. She had found this clump lying on the floor of my suite. I touch my head; I feel a blood-encrusted bald spot. I feel nauseated. Mike explains that he has already shown this gruesome piece of evidence to the police, who sealed it in a plastic bag and told him to make sure it goes in my luggage to Toronto with the rest of my packed belongings.

"It's time to go to the airport," Cathy says.

"Please, can someone find out if the papers are ready?" I ask.

"They don't have them, as yet. Maria told me they'll take them to the airport," Cathy says.

As I limp toward the jeep, I'm feeling totally powerless. Cathy and her friend, Randolph, assure me again that everything is all right. They seat me securely between them for the bumpy ride to the airport.

Liza, Steve, Anna Marie, and Mike promise that they'll make sure the papers get to me come hell or high water.

I'm grateful for these kind people as the jeep leaves the resort and turns onto the road to Santo Domingo.

I still don't understand how I managed to escape death. Looking back at all the horrors and the coincidences of this story, painstakingly documented in my leather binder lying by my bed, I believe that Providence stretched its protective hand over me for a purpose. It brought these wonderful Canadian people into my life. Their help, compassion, goodwill, and courage saved my life and proved to be indispensable later in my quest for justice.

Chapter 4. Nightmares in the Daylight!

"I've been trying to answer your question," I tell my psychologist, today. "Why didn't I see any sign of his violent nature, you asked? You know what? I don't think it was possible. Evil people seldom show their nature; crooks look honest, that's how they cheat people. Thieves often look decent and talk eloquently, so it's only after they get caught that we find out they are thieves. Some sophisticated crooks even climb to the top of a corporate ladder, deceiving not only their closest circle, but also the public at large. If only violent people could be recognized at first glance, they would have little opportunity to commit their atrocities. Providing someone was always nice to you and to others, how would you suspect him to be a violent hoodlum? And he was nice." I pause to shift my body in the armchair.

"Go on," the psychologist says.

I try to cross my legs, but one still hurts.

"Our relationship progressed quickly to mutual love and trust. There were many warm evenings at Harbourfront; dinners in restaurants; conversations, exchanged with words of love and compliments. One evening was particularly memorable. He arrived with two movies in his hand—a comedy and a drama—both films I'd been looking forward to seeing. I gave him a kiss and let him know that he made me happy.

"That evening, we were alone in my home. We dined outside under the patio umbrella in my backyard, with two lit candles between us.

"We seemed to like the same things—food, music, and movies.

"Normally, I'm more reserved, but I found myself immersed in the pleasure of this new relationship."

"That's all well," the psychologist intervenes, "so far as romance is concerned. Romantic feelings can mislead even the most suspicious character. Tell me a bit more about how your trust developed."

"Within a month, he introduced his daughter to me. It was when he had her on his visitation. I hear a little girl's voice protesting, 'Daddy! Daddy! Let me out of the car!'"

I run out to meet them. He greets me with his arms outstretched. My face is all smiles as I fall into his open arms, and he plunks a gentle kiss upon my cheek. He looks into my eyes.

"Hi, sweetie," he says.

I release myself from him, aware that his daughter is still in the back of the jeep.

"I want to get out, Daddy! Let me out, Daddy!"

"O.K., Anna." He opens the back door and reaches for her.

I watch him lift her from the car seat. She is beautiful. Her tiny four-year-old body clings tightly to him. Her curly, thick black hair and dark eyes sparkle. She smiles shyly.

"Anna, this is my friend, Marisha. Say hello to Marisha."

She is too shy to speak.

"Hello, Anna. What a beautiful name you have," I say.

She smiles and Ralph moves toward me for all of us to hug, but she protests, pushing us apart.

"Daddy! Daddy, stop it!"

I feel a bit strange but not offended. After all, if I were four years old, I would probably do the same.

"Who's that barking?" Ralph looks at Anna in mock surprise.

"Daddy! Daddy! Can I see the doggy?" Her eyes sparkle with joy.

"Sure, Anna."

He gently lets her down; she dashes toward the screen door.

"Daddy, can the doggy come out? I want to see him!"

"Of course, Anna!" He reaches down to pick her up in his arms.

I open the front door of my house, and Bito runs out. He's frantically tail wagging; Anna, in her father's arms, wriggles with glee.

"Daddy, let me down!" she cries out as she's trying to pull away from the embrace of Ralph's arms. He holds her back.

"Let Marisha show you how to pet Bito."

I bend down to pet my shaggy dog, and Ralph releases Anna on the ground. Immediately, Bito sniffs her; she giggles and runs away, but then she turns back to the dog and pets him. Her laughter doesn't stop as they run in a circle, together. Ralph takes my hand into his; we watch Anna and Bito bond.

"Marisha wants to know if you want to go to the playground."

"Yes, Daddy. Yes. Can Bito come with us, too?"

"Sure, Anna."

"Yea! Yea! Yea!" She jumps up and down with her hands in the air.

Anna's happiness makes Ralph and me laugh, and we watch her heading straight for the swings.

"Daddy! Daddy! Push me on this swing!" She laughs, the higher he pushes her. "Daddy, I want Marisha to push me, now."

She likes me. She giggles each time I touch her feet, then stretches her body forward as she tries to swing higher.

"I want to climb to the top!" she says. The swing stops; she jumps off and runs toward the playhouse. "To the top of the castle!"

That first day, she conquers all the playground equipment.

Back at home, Ralph helps me carry down the treasure chest. I give Anna some toys to play with, toys that belonged to my daughters many years ago. This brings back sweet memories. Anna's big brown eyes double with amazement, and I'm happy, too, seeing my children's toys played with once again.

Suddenly, she turns to her father.

"Marisha is my friend," she says.

He hugs her, and she encircles his leg with her little arms. I get down on my knees to meet her eye-to-eye.

"Yes, Anna, you're my new little friend, too." I squeeze her, gently.

She jumps up, giggles, and gives me a huge hug. I smile.

At this moment, if a stranger could see us, we would surely appear as a family.

"Is that all?" the psychologist asks.

"No. There was much more than that," I respond. "One evening, before leaving, he asks me to join him and his parents at a festival."

"So you thought that this meant that the relationship was getting serious?"

"Yes. Family is what life is all about."

"Tell me about meeting his parents."

It was a Sunday afternoon. Katrina, my mother, and I were off to Toronto Island. My mother always enjoys the ferry ride there. Today, she comments on the beautiful city skyline; its scrapers recede as the ferry crosses Lake Ontario to the island.

Twenty minutes later we step onto the island. The fanning effect of the lake breeze stops and the hot air hits like a wave. The crowd is typical of the vast cultural mosaic of the city. I hear so many dialects and distinguish the many languages. Roller bladders skirt along paths; Frisbee chasers slice through the open grassy fields; children run with kites; fathers bounce balls with their little ones. And, so we're entertained by people as we stroll along the beautiful lush green island.

The pond with the swan boats appears on the left. My mom hesitates for a moment because she knows that we'll insist on taking her for a ride. Katrina grabs her grandmother by the arm and leads her to a pink-coloured swan at the dock.

I take out my camera and wait for the perfect scene. I love these moments and today I feel happy, as I click a few shots that span three generations. However, in the back of my mind I'm eagerly awaiting the first meeting of Ralph's parents and my mom.

Katrina and my Mom end their swan ride. I snap another memorable shot, Katrina holds my mother's hand giving her assistance as she steps back onto the dock. I lean towards my Mom and give her a bear hug. She giggles whenever I squeeze her. I do that on purpose; she likes it.

At her age, my mother has a great deal of discomfort when she walks. I suggest to Katrina that she go on ahead to save us a park bench near the food kiosk. My mother sighs when she reaches the bench. When we are comfortably seated, with food and drink in our hands, my mother, as always, begins to tell us about the book she's reading. It's a history of the Tudor period in England this time. She could never understand why the English king kept so many wives locked up in the tower! I shrug my shoulders with a silent smile; how else could the king have kept so many wives faithful and enjoyed everyone of them?

My mind drifts as I think how blessed we are to have each other. We may not be a large family, here in Canada, but what we lack in size we make up in love.

At the city docks, Katrina leaves us and continues with her plans for the evening. My mother has agreed to accompany me to the Italian festival at Coronation Park.

The sound of Italian music drifting on the cool breeze announces that the festivities have already begun. Mom and

I head toward the designated meeting area. My heart skips as I see Ralph standing behind his seated parents. When Ralph sees me, he waves for us to come over. My mother likes his mom's Italian pronunciation of their shared name—"Maria".

"I'm happy your daughter likes my son Raffaele," his mother smiles.

I look at Ralph and with a smile I say to him, "I like your Italian name. Is it okay if I call you by it?"

"Sure, sweetie," he says and kisses me on the cheek.

Since our parents are getting along quite well, Raffaele and I decide to take a walk. Hand in hand we stroll a short distance from the crowd, but remain close enough to hear a romantic ballad pouring from the stage behind us.

My attention is on the psychologist now as she asks, "So you thought he treated his parents well "Throughout summer we shared a wonderful time with our immediate family members. There was no sign of any violence. On weekdays, Katrina and her boyfriend joined us for an occasional dinner, along with the exchange students. Then, every second Sunday when he had Anna visiting, I joined him for dinner at his parents' place. These family gatherings fostered our intimacy and confirmed our trust. His mother even invited us to her home for her birthday, an intimate Italian gathering—just 11 of us."

After the party Raffaele drives me to the heart of the city by the waterfront. There, he surprises me with an evening boat cruise.

The sunset reflects on glistening Lake Ontario. We dance under the starry skies; we lean on the railing of the boat while staring at the city lights. After the cruise, we drive to the East End Beaches, where we kick off our shoes, dig our toes into the cool sand, and sing together.

My session with the psychologist is almost over.

"You have a lot to cope with, Marisha," she says, pausing momentarily to look into my eyes. Then she resumes, "But in time, you will heal your physical and mental wounds. Luckily, you are a woman of strong character." She nods and again waits to see if I have something to say, but I'm listening, and she continues.

"Let me ask you this: What bothers you the most now? Is it the loss of this love, which ended so . . . traumatically? Or would you say, your physical health, or your present mental anxiety, or is it something else?"

"Something else!"

Chapter 5. No Protection at Home!

Today, on the way to her home Dana decides to visit me. She calls but my phone is busy. She stops anyway, unexpectedly. She wants to see my tan, but is she surprised! Dana remembers our trip to Dominican, the sand and the sea of the Caribbean Islands. How we found it difficult to leave the tropical sun, to return to the snow, salt, and sleet of our winters.

When Dana enters my home, she's devastated.

"What happened to you, Marisha?" she asks.

"Dana, it's a long story."

I'm tired of recollecting the attack, but I let her know the horrid details of the Cuban holiday. She keeps taking long deep breaths, completely speechless. Her elbows are propped on my living room table with her upper body leaning forward. I wish to hear something encouraging, but her eyes are filled with horror. I continue.

"Dana, that last day of vacation in Cuba, instead of lifting my face to absorb the last rays of the hot sun before returning to the cold, I slump in the backseat of the jeep and bury my scarred face in a handful of tissues."

"Were you alone at this time? Who helped you?"

So I tell her how I returned to Canada.

I am totally dependent on Cathy and Randolph. They carry me between them from the jeep and guide me through the crowd gathered in front of the busy airport. Inside they lower me into an empty seat in the waiting area. I can't stomach running into him! Cathy tells me that the Cuban authorities are detaining him until departure. I remember that her friend Randolph brought me a wheelchair. They whisk me to a private area near the departure lounge, away from the noise and the public stares.

When they wheel me in to the customs counter, the Cuban official gives me a long look after Cathy hands my passport to him. I feel very uncomfortable; he keeps glancing at my passport, peers back at my face, and then again stares on my photo.

"Is this you, Signora?" he asks in Spanish.

His question catches me off guard; I'm too stunned to answer.

"Of course, it's her passport," Cathy frowns at him.

He glares down at me in the wheelchair, and then scans the passport again. Tears fill my eyes and I start to wail. Randolph hands him my Ontario driver's license and my health card. The official asks us to wait.

"We better get Maria here, right away!" Randolph turns to Cathy.

She nods and leaves immediately. The medication starts to wear off and the pain seeps through hard. When Cathy returns, she tells us that Maria has disappeared and I swallow more painkillers. I let them know that I feel very insecure about leaving Cuba without the police declaration in my possession.

We're waiting for the immigration official, who seems to take forever to return. Randolph, very frustrated, paces back and forth for some time, then without a word, he leaves the room. Cathy and I figure that he has gone to search for Maria. I doze off again until the creaking wheels below me are in motion and I hear Maria speaking in Spanish behind me.

Cuban airport security officers lead us to a room with floor-to-ceiling glass windows overlooking the airport runway. The room is empty except for the customs and immigration officials, who brought us here, and a few security guards, dressed in blue uniforms, who are speaking loudly at the entrance near the large glass windows.

"Signora, you'll be more comfortable in here," one of the officials explains in broken English. When the two of them leave the room, everyone becomes quiet.

I'm more and more worried about which will arrive first, the declaration papers or the airplane. Without the papers, I will feel completely lost. The tears start again, pouring down my face. Cathy turns to Maria.

"Maria, so where are the declaration papers?" she asks.

Maria hesitates for a few seconds.

"They should be arriving any minute, now," she says in a thick Spanish accent. "I'll check on them, again." She turns and walks away.

I pause, as my mother brings us tea and a snack for Dana. She nods and waves her hands, anticipating the rest of my story, and asks,

"So what happened? Did you get the documentation?"

"Dana, it took hours for the plane to arrive," I tell her and then continue on about the fiasco trying to obtain the declaration.

I remember lying stretched out on a bench and Cathy trying to clean my face. She tells me that I dropped off to sleep two hours ago.

"Has Maria returned with the papers?" I keep demanding.

"Not yet," she shakes her head, "but Randolph has gone looking for her."

We are silent, but I feel desperation when Randolph appears without the papers and announces that the officials want us to use the other exit because the arrivals will be coming through here anytime. I'm terrified.

"Dana, I was traumatized by the attack and feeling like I was not going to make it back to Canada. The Cubans just wanted me to leave their country and without any documentation of the assault." I cry out.

Dana places her hand on my arm and comforts me.

"How terrible, Marisha, of what you had to go through! You know, the Cubans are smart. The last thing they want is to have the arriving vacationers see a battered departing tourist."

"As Cathy kept comforting me that Maria would fax the documentation to me in Canada, Randolph followed the officials' direction and wheeled me away from the arriving vacationers, toward the airplane. Dana, I thought, how will that be possible, since Maria doesn't have my fax number?"

"They just wanted you to leave Cuba, Marisha!" Dana concludes. I take up again, telling Dana more.

The closer we approach the airplane, the more I feel terrified. I keep telling them my confusing thoughts: Perhaps I should stay in Cuba until they provide me with the documentation. Cathy and Randolph keep assuring me that Liza and Steve will make sure the papers get to me. Anxiety overcomes me because I know that *he* is returning on the same airplane. I fear that if I see him I'll scream and go into shock.

Cathy enters first. I cling to her from behind and try to take a few steps at a time. I wobble, but Randolph steadies me and manages to get me to my seat.

It's difficult to sit upright; my stomach is swollen with gas from the medication. God knows what they have been giving me. I'm totally traumatized; flashbacks of the attack flood my mind. Cathy gives me another sedative and holds my hand.

There's no pill for my despair. It seems impossible that my loving relationship with Raffaele ended so tragically. I can't control the mental images of the attack. I drift away again, no idea for how long.

Cathy keeps me awake, explaining that many of the resort's vacationers gave her their contact numbers. She shows me the notes.

"Marisha, they're eager to testify about what he has done to you. Marisha, listen to me," Cathy adds. "You must contact them as soon as you can in Canada." She does not stop repeating, "When we land, as soon as the captain hands him over to the police, you must speak out and point to him and tell them that you charge Raffaele Grecci for assaulting you in Cuba."

Dana's dark eyes fill with tears.

"Wow, Marisha. I can't believe what you have gone through on your vacation!"

"Dana, now I am back in Canada, in my wonderful homeland, where justice, law, and order rule the nation. Am I safe? Will he be arrested and put in jail? Guess what, Dana? At Pearson International, I'm surrounded by the police, whose motto is 'To Serve and Protect.' However, I was traumatized; I could not charge him!"

"Wow! Unbelievable!"

"I couldn't believe it either, Dana. I just had to sit there and watch him walk away free! Dana, the police officers wouldn't even take me to the hospital; they only wheeled me to the passenger pickup area, handed me a Kleenex, and pointed to a courtesy phone."

"That's horrible! So how did you manage on your own?"

"Do you want to call home?" they asked.

"My first instinct is to dial my home number, but only then do I realize that Katrina and Dan have left for a vacation to Mexico. My mother doesn't drive. Dana, I did not want to call you and disturb you in the middle of the night, and Ruth had gone on a vacation as well, so I dial Monica. Her husband, Sal, answers, and puts Monica on the phone. Monica immediately asks, 'What's wrong Marisha? Where are you?'"

"I'm stranded at the airport." I burst into tears.

"What happened, Marisha? What happened?"

"Please, come and get me, please."

"We'll be right there. We'll be there as soon as we can."

What a sight I am; passersby gawk at me—an injured woman, left all alone by the curb in a wheelchair. I try to hide my face, and hope for my friends' speedy arrival.

"What happened?" Sal asks.

"Where's Raffaele?" Monica demands.

"He's the one that did this to me."

"But . . . we just saw you both before Christmas. You were so happy together!" Monica says.

"I can't believe he has done this to you," Sal adds, "Let's go. The car is over here."

I don't recall much of our conversation but only that Monica and Sal kept asking me, "Did you charge him?"

Dana wants to know, as well, she leans forward and eagerly asks,

"So did you charge him?"

"In Cuba, but I can't charge him here in Canada. Authorities just told me there's no law in Canada to protect me."

"So, where else can you charge him? He's a Canadian. He's committed this brutality upon you. And, you're also a Canadian," Dana declares. "You need to get a restraining order, immediately!" she adds strongly.

"No! They told me it's impossible!"

"That's incredible!" Dana yells. "You've got to be kidding me! There's nothing to protect you?" she adds and frowns at me.

I wait for her to calm down; my mother pours some more tea for us. I continue telling Dana about my return to Canada from a holiday in hell experience.

"From the back seat, I kept asking Monica for Kleenex. They were not sure what to do since there was blood dripping, continuously, out of my mouth and nose. Sal decided to take me to the closest hospital, York Central.

At the hospital Sal and Monica hail an attendant and wheel me into an examination room. Nurses scurry around for IV bottles. I wasn't feeling too good about this. They inserted a tube into my arm.

Finally, when I wake up, I'm still on the hospital bed but now in Canada. My mind races; why am I here? I look down at my body and see bandages wrapped around my chest, neck, and upper arms. I touch my face. More bandages. I feel like damaged goods and wonder what I will say to my students. My first impulse is to get out of the hospital. But a nurse, passing by my bed, stops my inept attempt to sit up.

"You'll have to remain here until the tests are done," she says.

The sights and smells of the hospital irritate me. Everyone seems to stare at me; I don't want my suffering on display. Their shocked expressions make me want to cover myself with the sheets when I hear people whisper.

I keep pressing the emergency button. No one comes. I fidget. I notice a phone and I dial Raffaele's work number. He answers. I have difficulty forming words.

"How . . . how could you do this to me?" I stutter.

"How did God allow this to happen to you?" He replies, harshly.

His words fill me with disgust. I squeeze the phone until my fingers sting and try to rein in my galloping heart.

"My scars may disappear, but my spirit will not heal until I get justice for what you did to me! How am I supposed to go on with my life? How can I return to teaching, like this, today or tomorrow?"

"I don't know," he responds.

"I will make sure you don't get away with this," I say.

"Please. I'll get you some money. Whatever you want."

His response disgusts me. I hang up the phone. My anger toward him consumes me. It drives me to contact his parents.

"What a son you have raised! He has . . ." I tell her how her son has almost killed me.

"Oh, my God," his mother yells.

"What has he done, now?" I can hear his father shout in the background.

I hear his mother and father screaming, I'm terrified by their outbursts, and I feel that they will not help me, now, so I slam down the phone.

Dana straightens her body with an expression of disgust.

"What a beast!" Dana yells.

"Dana, I should have known the call would accomplish nothing. Perhaps the victim always wants to extract a word of remorse from the attacker. But my attacker was supposed to have loved me! What a cruel joke!"

"He's an awful man to do this to you!" Dana twists again, "So when did you get home from the hospital?"

"I don't remember exactly when. The hospital's crisis unit asked me some questions. I told the social worker, 'I've had too many shocks for one day.' Debra, the worker,

explained to me that I must contact the crisis unit as soon as
I can."

"Did you get the results from the hospital?" Dana
asks.

"Before I left, the doctor brings in the report
documenting the results: a deep laceration to the nose—it's
fractured and deviated to the left; a cut under the right eye
and on the upper-left lip; and there's a possible spinal
injury. I have to wait for MRI results. I'm to make an
appointment with my family doctor to take out the
stitches."

"That's good, Marisha," she says and then adds, "So
how long were you at the hospital?"

"A day or more, I think. The ward was crowded and I
just wanted to get out of there. I drifted back into sleep."

My mother's head is bowing down now, so I reach for
her hand, she acknowledges my touch with a nod. I resume
telling Dana, practically stuttering, about my first day upon
return from my holiday.

"Dana, I woke up a strong hand was resting over my
forehead. Through my functioning eye, I see my mother.
My mother's arm was heavily laden with a paper bag filled
with my Cuban X-rays, my test results from the Emergency
Department, and my new prescriptions. She wheeled me
through the automatic doors of the hot hospital out into the
cold winter air. I still feel the bright sunlight reflecting from
the snow stinging my eye."

I pause, feeling the love of my mother's hand holding
mine. Dana sips her tea; my mom offers her the snacks.

"I hate to ask you this question, but why do you suppose Raffaele behaved this way?"

"Dana, my mind races; I'm searching for the reason why he attacked me. Except, he behaved differently and was unjustly jealousy right at the beginning of the vacation."

"This must be difficult for you to understand. But how are you going to charge him?"

When Dana repeats the words "How are you going to charge him?" my hostility overrides my usual good social graces.

"How should I know? There's no law for this crime! No one cares to protect me!"

Dana knows that my tropical vacation with Raffaele has created pure hell for me.

"There has to be a way!"

She's sympathetic and encouraging; however, the kind of help I need she cannot provide. She sees me like never before, with no peace.

We sit in silence. Hundreds of paranoid thoughts get past the cobwebs from the concussion and the medication.

"Since this trip, Dana, I am asking myself over and over, 'Were the last six months of my life one big charade? Did he know that he could get away with this? The police must have made a mistake at the airport! Is there really no law to protect me?'"

Dana interrupts, "I'm completely bewildered by our laws!!"

"I am horrified!!" I stutter.

"Did he plan it? What can you do? Marisha, he could try to hurt you, again. Is there really no law to protect you?"

"Dana, what will I do, now?"

Dana does not have any answers. She leaves exhausted and confused, telling me that she'll pray for the situation.

***

My cuddly dog, Bito, stubbornly refuses to leave the house without me. I nudge him. I know that my mother is overtired, but I still suggest that she and Bito go out for a bit of air. He squeals, looks back at me, and drags on the leash. When they are gone, I am back to my troubles. I still need to know the status of my paperwork from Cuba. Although I realize that I am not in any state to conduct a long-distance conversation in Spanish, I grab the phone. To my surprise, I get through right away to the resort hotel.

"Buenos dias."

"Do you speak English?" I ask.

"Uno poco, Signora. How can I help you?"

"I need to speak to Maria. It's a matter of great 'urgencia.'"

"Un momentigo, por far vor. Just a minute, please. I call her for you." She puts me on hold. I browse through the files, but I can't concentrate. My eyes start to close, and I begin drifting off to sleep when a voice finally comes on the phone.

"This is Maria, director of Alba Tours. How may I help you?"

"Maria, this is Marisha Manley." I try to sit up, so I can sound more alert, but the pain is too much. "Maria, he was not charged at the airport, as promised. And I'm still waiting for the Cuban police report."

"You mean he was not arrested in Canada?"

"No! Maria, please fax me the papers, immediately."

"I'm shocked. I had no knowledge of this," she says.

I already doubt her veracity. After all, out of sight, out of mind. Logically, her first interest is keeping the resort full of happy Canadian tourists. I am afraid she wants to try to sweep away the incident to avoid involving the resort hotel in any legal repercussions.

"Maria, please give Steve and Liza the paperwork. They are still at the resort. Can you put me through to them?"

"They have gone to Santiago for the day. I'll have them call you, when they return."

"Please, Maria. It's urgent."

"I will."

I hang up abruptly and hope that I have made my point.

When the expected call doesn't arrive that evening, my despair alternates with anger. Without this documentation I can't obtain a restraining order. My heart palpitates. Everything I eat or drink passes right through my system.

At the end of the day, the phone rings. It's Steve and Liza.

"Marisha, what's going on?" Steve asks.

"I can't charge him here in Canada." I start to cry.

"What? You've got to be joking."

I try to speak, but my sobbing obliterates my words.

"Because it happened in Cuba," I manage to say. My stutter moves an octave higher. "The police told me they have no jurisdiction to charge him in Canada."

"Un-be-lie-va-ble! The son of a bitch must have known he could get away with it! When the Cubans found out what he did to you, they wanted to take him to the mountains! This is unfucking real!"

"Steve, I'm not sure that Maria is working on the declaration papers. I need them right now. I need to get a restraining order against him."

"Hang in there, Marisha! I will damn well make sure she does! Here's Liza."

"Marisha, I can't believe it! I thought he'd be handcuffed right at the airport."

"It's not good, Liza."

"We'll call you tomorrow, as soon as Maria has the papers ready to fax."

I collapse back on the bed. My anger exceeds my pain. He's not going to get away with this. But how? My mind searches over and over, but no immediate resolution pops up.

I lift my head off the pillow and reach for a pen on my bedside table. I'm thinking that there's nothing more conductive to fear than inaction. I pick up the pen and my journal lying on my bedside and begin to scrawl. I swear to God I'll document exactly what happened to me in Cuba, just in case I'm not around to tell my story. I record all events beginning at the start of that trip in December.

***

During the next day, I continue documenting my ongoing ordeal.

January 7, 1999, I note in my journal:

Today, I wake up with a migraine headache. My face, my neck, my shoulders, and back are aching. Even the palms of my hands hurt. I've just woken up, but I feel like going to sleep again.

I put down my pen. Anger erupts, again. Damn it! No psychopathic idiot is going to get away with the brutal crime he has committed against me!

My telephone startles me. I nearly step on my dog lying at my bedside.

"Hello," I say into the receiver.

"Can I speak to Marisha Manley?" a strong, polite official voice asks.

"This is she."

"This is Sergeant Cooper from Peel Regional Police Department. I'm calling to see if you need any assistance or information concerning legal aid or counseling."

"Counseling? I'm scared. You've released a homicidal manic back on the street without any repercussions and you refer me, the victim, to counseling?"

"I'm truly sorry, ma'am, but our hands are tied. This is beyond our jurisdiction. I can give you a number for the legal aid. Perhaps if you speak to a lawyer, he can shed some light on your situation."

"What I need is a restraining order to protect me from my attacker, not a lawyer. I'm scared he'll kill me!"

"I'm sorry; we're unable to do anything. I can give you a number to contact the Justice of the Peace. Perhaps, they can help."

The word "perhaps" irritates me; I think I've heard it too many times lately. I take down the numbers given to me, thinking that as soon as I have the documents from Cuba, I'll have to do everything to obtain a restraining order against Raffaele.

***

It's four in the afternoon; I still haven't heard from Steve and Liza. I remind myself that they were kind people who genuinely helped me in my time. Why wouldn't they continue to do so now?

Another short ring on my phone indicates it's a local call. It's Sheri, Dan's mother.

"How was your trip?" she asks.

Usually, I give her a happy, exuberant monologue. Her simple question makes me shake because she's about to become the next person in my life privy to my nightmare.

"Sheri, I'm not well."

"What's the matter? You have a cold?"

"Sheri, can you please come over as soon as you can?"

She tells me she'll be here right away.

I'm surprised at how fast she arrives. My mother greets her at the door. I hear Sheri cry out, "Why? Why? Why?" over and over again.

I can hear her wailing voice from upstairs, but I'm too weak to say anything. By the time she arrives by my bedside, she's shaking uncontrollably. She covers her mouth, and she cries with a sound I have never heard before. She folds her arms around me, rocking me without letting go for a long time; her long, black hair damp with tears hangs over my face.

"Oh, Marisha. What did he do? How could he?" She pulls her hair back. Her luminous Persian eyes fill with anger. "How could he do this to you? We just saw you on Christmas. Everything was great. What happened to him? Do Katrina and Dan know this?"

"No."

There's a long deadly silence.

"Where is he now?" she asks in a quiet voice.

I tell her more of what has transpired in the last two days.

"Incredible!" She adds, "What a monster!"

She brushes off my attempt to tell her about legal complications.

"Marisha, I'm concerned for your safety." Her dark face turns a shade lighter; she fidgets, looks at my mother, and continues. "Imagine, you can be murdered by your husband in Cuba, and he comes back as a free man." As she leaves, Sheri assures me that she is available 24 hours a day. "Don't be afraid to ask for help."

In the middle of Sheri's hysteria, I'm relieved to discover my mother's strength. I write in my journal:

My mother's calmness is the glue that is holding my life together these days!

In the morning, my mother beats me to the long phone ring. I hope it's from Cuba.

"It's Liza! Pick up the phone," she shouts from downstairs.

"Liza, so nice to hear your voice."

"Marisha, how are you doing?"

"I wish I could say 'good.' But to tell you the truth, Liza, there's no progress. To this day I don't have any paperwork from Cuba to protect myself in Canada."

"No? That's impossible. Maria swore that she'd fax them to you."

"I understood that she was giving them to you."

"Maria explained that the paperwork will take the police longer because the case is international."

I suddenly realize that Liza and her husband, my newfound vacation friends, have, in less than two short weeks, extended to me an extraordinary kindness. I feel humbled.

"I'll talk to Maria, again. We'll bring the photos as soon as we're home," she says.

How can I burden this family on their vacation any further? It would be immoral.

Chapter 6. Trauma vs. Romance

"Something else." The psychologist picks up my remark at the end of the previous session. "That's your security, isn't it?"

"Yes, for sure," I say emphatically. "Unfortunately no psychologist can help me with that. Neither law nor the police can protect me. Victimized, sick and helpless, how am I supposed to survive?"

"Hold on, Marisha. Under any circumstance, you have to find strength to calm down, as fear and worry never help, but make things worse. We will deal with this issue, as well as the post-traumatic effect. Tell me, have you told me everything about Raffaele and relations with him? Are you sure that his love was genuine? Are you sure that there was no indication of his violent character?"

"Regarding love . . . ," I said, trying to see our romance from a different angle.

It was in October, the month of my birth, when fall transforms the greenery of summer into a vibrant array of blazing colors. The trees, the grass, and the flowers together emit an incandescent power, their shapes igniting into burning configurations, slowly shedding their colors to carpet the earth's bed.

During autumn, some part of nature dies; some parts come alive. Every season encircles the other, giving its own gifts to the world. Raffaele's love for me seems evergreen. He continually demonstrates it in so many different ways. I'm overwhelmed   by the promise of what is ahead of me.

"Happy birthday, Sweetheart," Raffaele calls out from the driveway. The awesome roses he's carrying hide his face.

"Thank you, Raffaele." I can barely hold the flowers as I lean forward to seal my words with a gentle kiss on his lips.

The scent of the roses permeates my entire home.

That day I decide to surprise Raffaele's mother with a large bouquet from my birthday roses. I'm about to ring the doorbell when I hear Raffaele shouting harshly in Italian. I wait a moment, hoping that the yelling will stop. I have no idea what is being said. I timidly ring the doorbell and the shouting comes to a sudden halt. Raffaele's mother opens the door. She is dabbing her dark eyes. I hug her and hand her the large bouquet of flowers. I ask if she's all right. She responds by telling me she has to have surgery on her wrist, next Wednesday. Raffaele appears from the next room, his face flushed, with beads of sweat pouring down his temples. I approach him.

"Are you all right?" I ask.

He responds by telling me that it was just a silly family misunderstanding concerning his daughter. He explains that his parents are very upset about the arrangement regarding the visitations with Anna. I want to know more, but Raffaele says that it is nothing to worry about and quickly changes the subject by telling me that he has another surprise for me this evening. My visit with Raffaele and his parents is short. I step into the car. I'm surprised as I hear the shouting begin, again. I drive off, thinking I must speak to him about it.

At seven he arrives at my home, and I again ask him if he's all right because I heard more shouting between him and his parents when I left their house. He assures me again that it was nothing to worry about. He quickly goes on to tell me about the special birthday dinner he has planned for us tonight. I want to know more about the argument, but I decide not to ask. I hurry up the stairs, put on my best dress, and fix my hair. I'll ask him about this later.

He's standing at the bottom of the stairs, eyes wide open, when he sees me.

"You always look beautiful, but tonight you look amazing!"

I laugh, pinching his side as we walk to his jeep and drive away.

We arrive at a beautifully lighted old building. The trees lining the path toward the entrance glisten with tiny festive lights. We enter through heavy wooden doors into the large dining area, its many rooms separated by etched glass panels. Crystal stemware, shimmering chandeliers, and tiny white lights enhance the baroque antique décor. The ambiance is romantic, but the place is slightly over the top for my taste.

The maitre d' greets us. My senses dance as we follow him through the restaurant. Two-tone roses make up each table centrepiece; white candles cast their warm light upon the patrons.

Our waitress awaits us.

"Welcome," she says. Her red mouth shines like cherry jam; her eyebrows are plucked to thin curves. She quickly removes the RESERVED sign from the table. "Can I bring you an aperitif?"

"Aqua fresca, please," Raffaele says, as she walks away as quickly as she can in her tight black dress.

From the inside pocket of his dark suit, Raffaele pulls out a golden box tied with a fancy red lace ribbon. He places it in front of me.

"Try to guess what's inside this box." He smiles.

I'm caught off-guard by his question, a bit tongue-tied, as the returning waitress interrupts us.

"Have you decided what you'll have tonight?" she asks.

"No. Not yet." Raffaele replies.

She pours the water into our glasses and leaves immediately.

"Umm, let's see," I say as I take the box. "Well, the box is too big for a ring."

He laughs. I pick up the box and shake it a bit.

"Oh, wait a minute, it has a bit of weight, and it rattles, too." I laugh. "It's the world's smallest toaster."

He laughs and picks it up.

"Let me help you," he says. "However, first close your eyes. No peeking, now."

I'm waiting with anticipation. I feel his hands touching my fingers and then he places something on my wrist.

"Open your eyes, please," he says.

I open my eyes to see a tennis bracelet of diamonds encircling my wrist. I look up at him lovingly.

"Oh, Raffaele, it's beautiful!"

"I want to show you my love is forever." He smiles. "I feel that if it doesn't work out between us, it will not work with anyone else."

After sipping cognac, we head to the ballroom where a live band plays a mix of upbeat oldies and semi-jazzy tunes. Then, Raffaele asks the musicians if they would let him do a song for me, on my birthday. He serenades me with a cute but shaky rendition of *Te Amore*.

Raffaele tells me how lucky he is to have found me and then asks me if I would consider buying a house with him. I respond to him that it's still too early in our relationship and that we have to consider our children. He smiles and responds,

"You're right."

"I will, Raphael."

I have no doubt his love for me is real. Love is good, I say to myself.

The psychologist nods in understanding.

"It seems that his feelings were genuine," she agrees. "Sometimes trifles can trigger uncontrollable outbursts of anger and violence in psychotic personalities though."

"In December Raffaele found a beautiful home close by. The first two weeks of this month, we decorate the three-bedroom house and prepare Anna's room, for whenever she'll be visiting. What could be more convincing?" Tears run down my cheeks.

"At that point, you weren't planning to go to Cuba?" she asks. I continue,

"True. I still was looking forward to Christmas in Canada."

Amidst the shopping frenzy, on the way to the café, Raffaele steers me toward the Marlin Travel Agency. The store window is filled with charming destinations, enticing the cold-weather-stricken Canadians to exotic getaways: "Cuba—Our warmth is contagious," I read and drift away in thought. The palm trees on the poster seem to move; their swaying beckons and I can almost feel the warm white sand beneath my feet. I wake from my brief trance.

"Your present is here, in this store," Raffaele says.

I'm a bit confused, since I have already told Raffaele that, at this point in time, an exotic trip is out of the question, since I'd already blown my budget on a ticket to visit my daughter, Daniella, in England.

"Hello, Mr. Grecci."

"Hi, Carmella, this is Marisha." Raffaele introduces me to the travel agent.

No doubt, he has spoken to her before; it seems he's made definite plans for us.

"Marisha, have you ever been to Cuba?" The deep voiced Italian woman smiles across her desk.

"Yes, I have," I smile back at her.

"I bet you have never been in this place. It's a fantastic all-inclusive resort laid out on a long, sprawling beach, in a very unspoiled corner of Cuba. You'll love it there."

I'm slightly dumbfounded by his presenting me with a Christmas gift of this magnitude in a public place.

"Marisha, I want to take you to Cuba."

I feel a bit shy that he announces this in front of the woman. I wish we were in a more private place; I wish he had just handed me the ticket so that perhaps I could express my gratitude to him with a kiss, but now with the woman starring at me I just resort to a smile. "We're going to Cuba for the New Year? Raffaele, this is fantastic!"

"This is my gift to you, Marisha."

"Thank you, Raffaele," I say, kissing him.

An uncontrollable cough interrupts my stream of words. I realize that my psychologist spends too much time with me, but I am the last patient today; she understands that in telling her my story, I unconsciously unload a heavy burden from my mind.

"Take your time, Marisha," she said, stretching a paper tissue to me. "From what you have said so far, it is inconceivable to expect such violence from a loving person. His angry argument with relatives is certainly not an indicator. Shouting and yelling happens sometimes in the most peaceful families. Perhaps something more troublesome happened in Cuba before his violent attack?"

"Your guess is correct. That's how it was."

We're finally departing his place for our Cuban holiday. I'm bubbling with excitement, anticipating the adventure that awaits us, but Raffaele nervously smokes one cigarette after another all the way to the airport. I'm wondering if he has a fear of flying. In retrospect, it seems weird, but nothing remarkable happened during the flight.

On the bus ride through the Cuban countryside from the airport to the resort, we converse with two young ladies who both work in tourism. We're pleased when they tell us how great Marre Del Portillo is, great food, lots of activities, and the live entertainment is brilliant.

"We love it here. It's our third time," Meagan, the more outgoing of the two says. "You guys will have a ball!"

In the distance, a brightly painted resort spreads out along a white sandy beach, and on a hill, through the thick, lush greenery, a high-rise oval hotel pops up. The loud meringue music intensifies as the bus stops in front of the beige and pink gates. Staff members line up on both sides of a long burgundy carpet leading to the doors of the resort, and then they greet us, one by one. Each vacationer receives a colourful necklace of flowers. The friendly people, the hot weather, the incredible azure water, and the sunny sky create an amazing first impression.

The porter takes our bags to our ocean view suite. We open them quickly; throw on beach clothing, and in our bare feet head straight to the shoreline. The sun's rays lure me to the water. I dive into the foamy waves.

"Raffaele, the water's great! Come on, jump in!" I wave to him.

"I'll be right back," he says, returning my wave and pointing toward the beach bar. He sits down there and mingles with other tourists.

The clear, warm water of the Caribbean quickly washes away the Canadian cold. I dip my head back and smooth my hair. As each wave washes over me, I feel a surge of renewal.

The resort is perfect. The first evening's dinner, punctuated with Latin music and just the right amount of tropical evening breeze, creates an incredibly romantic atmosphere. One set into the Welcome Night Revue, trouble slithers into paradise.

As the night unfolds its starry canopy over the resort's outdoor music festivities, we sip piña coladas with a group of fellow Canadians. Raffaele sits quietly, except for yelling in broken Spanish at the waiter to bring him another drink. Just before the band begins to play its second set, an entirely different Raffaele suddenly emerges—a side of him I had never witnessed before. Suddenly, anger erupts from him like a volcano. He shouts profanities at me in front of three Canadian ladies seated across from us at our table. Fortunately, they don't understand obscenities sworn in Italian. The embarrassment caused by his behaviour is nothing compared to the sting in my heart.

It's as though he swallowed the potion that turned Dr. Jekyll into Mr. Hyde. I'm shocked, embarrassed, and appalled. I hold onto the table to steady myself. The three women stare speechlessly at the scene. I get up from the table and run to the cabana.

I splash my face with cold water. Raffaele walks in.

"Why were you starring at them?" he asks.

"What do you mean? Starring at whom?"

"You know who. The singer in the band," he says as he grabs my arm and throws me to the floor.

I bang my head and knee on the hard marble. Shocked and stunned, I am unable to pick myself up. He continues to shout insults at me as he paces the room. I get up, bolt for the door, dash to the front desk, and beg the manager to move me to another suite.

The following day, I'm still in shock and puzzled as to what came over him. How could his behaviour change so suddenly? The only time I ever saw him angry or even raise his voice was at his family's house, the afternoon of my birthday. At that time, I did not understand the context, but now, when I think back on it, the emotion was definitely anger.

I feel so hurt that I approach Maria, the tourist coordinator, to see if she can arrange a flight back to Toronto, immediately.

"I'm sorry, the next flight is in four days," she says.

I decide to make the best of the situation and perhaps talk out the problem with Raffaele, but not right away.

The following morning, while having breakfast at poolside, Liza, her husband, Steve, and their two preteen children join me. In search of a playmate, Kyle, the older of the two, invites me to play a game of Scrabble. As we're into the first two words of the game, Raffaele approaches. He sits down at the table and begins to apologize, profusely, ignoring the presence of the youngster. He's embarrassing me, but I try not to shun him completely, so I agree to meet with him the following morning.

The next day he approaches me around 11 AM and suggests a walk on the beach. Because many people have already gathered there, I agree. We walk, slowly, two arms-lengths apart. He tries to justify his jealous outrage by telling me how much he loves me. He repeatedly promises that he'll never hurt me again.

I'm adamant about him understanding that he must never—ever—repeat that type of behaviour. I react very coolly. I explain that he has no right to direct this kind of anger toward me. I see him sweating more than usual; I wonder if it's the heat of the sun or the alcohol he consumed last night.

We walk up from the beach to the Caribe del Farrallon, our resort's sister hotel; it's already lunchtime. The only air-conditioned restaurant is filled to capacity. The maitre d' asks us if we would mind joining another couple. When I recognize the couple as Mike and Anna Marie, whom I met the day before, I am more than glad. Their presence is a welcome relief. They try to encourage us as a couple; Mike offers humorous anecdotes of their lives.

The four of us return to our resort. Anna Marie suggests that we take a side trip on Tuesday for a lobster dinner at a Cuban family's home.

"That sounds good; I'll get back to you later," I say.

I'm still not convinced of Raffaele's sincerity, plus I want him to think long and hard about what he did. I decide to remain cool and stay in my own room for now.

Over the next few days, Raffaele joins me in some of the resort activities, but always in the company of my new Canadian friends. At dinner, he joins Liza, Steve, their children, Anna Marie, Mike, and me at our table. In the few private moments that we share, Raffaele seems to show deep concern and love for me and remorse for his actions.

A group of us at the resort decides to take a full-day excursion on horseback through the beautiful Cuban countryside. Raffaele, who's afraid of horses, decides to tag along. His cavalier gesture warms my heart. During this trip we stop for a swim and a lunch break by a tropical waterfall, where Raffaele asks me when, if ever, I am coming back to him. However, at the end of the day, I still remain in my own suite.

73

Our fourth excursion is a bus tour to Santiago. Along with other tourists from our resort, we explore some of the most interesting historical sites. A group of us eats lunch on the upper deck of the Santiago Hotel, overlooking the old city's square below.

Throughout this day until we return to the resort, Raffaele tries very hard to show me his affection. He buys me a cute trinket—a woodcarving of a loving couple—emphasizing how he wants us to rebuild the solid relationship that we had started before this trip.

Then, late in the afternoon of New Year's Eve, he appears at my door with a porter beside him carrying his suitcases. He sweetly suggests that because it's New Year's Eve, would I be willing to give him another chance and a fresh start in the new year? I'm a little hesitant at first and taken aback by his bold move, but since he has treated me with respect and love, I break down and allow him to move into my suite.

New Year Eve is magical. We celebrate until dawn with our new friends. Raffaele and I are fast becoming a couple, again.

It's New Year's Day; a horse-drawn cart stops before our building. An old man with a squeaky voice calls from below, "Buenos dias, Signor, Signora!"

Overlooking the balcony, I see only a large straw hat and bony sun-dried hands holding the reigns of a horse as old as he.

"Uno momento, Signor," Raffaele replies and locks the door of the suite.

I plop my wide-brim sunhat on as we run down the stairs and climb onto the hot vinyl seats of the horse cart and clip-clop our way to the local village. In our state of happiness, we talk about yesterday's togetherness and future plans: Everything that is spoken about is accentuated by the words "us," "our," and "we."

"This will look great in our living room," Raffaele says when I pick up a sculpture from the local artisan's table; he's saying we are officially together, again, and I agree.

We return for a lobster lunch. The bulletin board announces many activities by the poolside; the social mingling has created a sort of Canadian ghetto. On our way to the swimming pool, a couple from Toronto walks with us. They invite us to visit them at their restaurant, *Milos,* on Danforth Avenue, when we return. A cheer from a nearby group activity drowns out our conversation; we thank them for their invitation and carry on.

Kiera, Liza's daughter, splashes water on us playfully.

"Come on, whales, catch us if you can," she says.

Raffaele and I dive in, pretending to capture them. The water sports wind down to a game of Scrabble with Kyle, and Raffaele joins Steve and Liza for horseshoes. We all reunite at the patio for a card game.

Raffaele and I dine alone this evening, with only candlelight between us; then we join the other vacationers who are already enjoying the musical show that imitates legends and celebrities such as Elvis Presley and Celine Dion. The evening ends with Raffaele and me dancing under the stars, then strolling, hand-in-hand, alone on the shore.

On our second-to-last day, Raffaele arranges a boat trip to a nearby island with a few other tourists. The old captain's toothless smile widens as he watches our laughter increase with every swell that splashes over the tiny boat's bow.

After a relaxing day of fishing, sunbathing, and eating fresh oysters, we return to our suite.

The next day is even better. It's clear to me that our intimacy and our communication are returning. I feel myself beginning to forgive him, and once again I feel swept away by his charm. I hope that I have made the right decision.

Dinner is served in the large dining room across from the pool. Tonight, an exposition of Cuban art surrounds the buffet, spread out from the middle to the four corners of the room. We dine with Anna Marie, Mike, Liza and Steve, and other new friends. Just before the night's festivities wind down, we say our goodnight and goodbyes; tomorrow morning, Raffaele and I return to Toronto, while our new friends remain here for another week.

But just as soon as we are inside our suite, the atmosphere changes, drastically.

"Mike has told me that you hugged him, inappropriately," he tells me.

I'm stunned by this accusation. I have no idea where this is coming from.

"This is ridiculous. It's not true," I swear to him.

I go on to tell him that if Mike feels that I have offended him in any way, I must speak to both of them, at once.

I quickly leave the room with Raffaele in tow. I knock on their door, and on the third rap Anna Marie answers. Immediately, I apologize for the late visit and, turning to Mike, I begin to explain. "Raffaele has brought to my attention that you told him that I have offended you, Mike. He says that I have hugged you inappropriately. Is this right?"

Anna Marie and Mike stand, dumbfounded. Mike is still, but Anna Marie's body is moving, nervously, as if waiting for a quick explanation.

"Absolutely not! You haven't offended me! This never happened!" Mike sternly states, and taking a few steps closer, he adds, "I have never said anything like this to you, Raffaele," looking him straight in the eye.

An uncomfortable silence hangs in their room. I am looking at Raffaele, who is staring at his shoes saying nothing but then walks up to me with stretched arms and hugs me; he quickly apologizes to Mike and Anna Marie. I am now totally overwhelmed. We leave their room, quickly.

Raffaele and I walk back up the stairs to my suite, silently. I am very upset that Raffaele created such an unpleasant incident, lied to me, and made Anna Marie and Mike a part of it. I just want to go to sleep. The horror and pain of a brutal beating wakes me up.

I finish my story and sigh, returning to the reality of the medical office.

"You're a strong woman, Marisha," the psychologist says. "Sooner or later, you'll recover your mental and physical health. But frankly, I think the clash with this psychopath was inevitable. This kind of person likes abusing others, and at the same time they are convinced that they are always right. They usually have exaggerated pride founded on nothing. They hate disobedience and objection. They hate strong personalities, particularly strong women. The apology to Mike and Anna Marie was the last devastating lesson for him. As every liar, who wants to look like a gentleman, he was outraged. He could have killed you just because you are a strong woman and do not tolerate bad behaviour and lies. But you did the right thing, Marisha. Now, by seeking justice, you do the right thing, too. There may be a problem in the Canadian law, but there is no such glitch in the minds of law-abiding citizens: They all believe that any crime, particularly a violent one, must be punished. Surely with your strong will, determination, and intelligence, you'll eventually get justice done concerning him. See you next week."

On the way home, I thought that eventually the law would reflect this simple point of view, which is the foundation of any civilized society and its fundamental understanding of justice.

Chapter 7. Shattered Life!

I relentlessly scrawl today's events in my journal.

January 7, 1999

My stress level is now at ten on the Prozac scale! On one hand, I'm depressed, without energy; on the other, the combination of confronting anxiety, fear, and uncertainty compels me to do the unlikely. I order an alarm to be installed in the house that I have raised my two daughters in for the last fifteen years!

I hate myself for displaying panic and fury. I even think of moving, but that would be a cowardly act. This is the house my children grew up in. It's their home. The neighbourhood is our community. Everyone knows us here. If I move, I abandon the essential principles of right and wrong, which are presently my only motivation to go on.

My hand slows down; my fingers are almost numb, and my pen wavers. At the end of the journal's page, I scribble some questions:

What to do, now? A lawyer! What lawyer? The only time I had a lawyer is the time I bought my house!

My pen drops out of my hand.

My mother and Bito are beside me. I welcome the moment when they both decide to take a walk. I feel safe with them, but I'm about ready to exchange my security for my intrinsic need for privacy. In the last 20 years, my mother and I have not been under the same roof for more than eight hours at a time.

There's a knock at the door. My neighbour, Shelley, is calling my name outside. I let her in with my head bowing to hide my injuries—an art I have already practised in front of the mirror. She almost drops the casserole dish that she has prepared for me.

Shelley has known me as her neighbour, a single mother with two grown daughters. I tutored her children and regard her as a casual acquaintance. I introduced her to him and his daughter. After that, Shelley saw us many times, when we, along with my dog, passed her house on the way to the neighbourhood park. Today, after she spoke to my mother on the street, I'm forced to allow her into my normally private life.

Shelley tells me that if I need anything, she'll be there for me. I appreciate her kindness without any expectations.

Repeated panic attacks fill my day. As an athlete my body knows pain, but constant headaches are something new to me.

Bad news travels fast. My phone doesn't stop ringing.

It's Ruth. I'm not sure she knows; she was on her vacation, but maybe Dana has already spoken with her. I let her speak first. Sure enough, she's in the loop.

"Marisha, I can't believe what he did to you! Don't worry, I'll talk to the lawyers here at my office and see whether or not he can be charged in Canada."

"Thanks, Ruthie. I really appreciate that."

She goes on to tell me that after being away, she's swamped with four partners' depositions at her law firm.

She promises to visit me as soon as she can. I feel relieved that she'll not have to see me in this condition.

"How did Ruth know about this?" I've already lectured my mother about discretion.

"I thought I told you earlier. She called, but you must have been asleep."

I lay down on the couch. My mother continues to follow the hospital's orders and insists on swabbing my stitches with an antibiotic ointment. She props my head up with another pillow and tells me that I need to keep my upper body elevated to decrease the swelling in my face.

I can't stand being helpless. As I drift into sleep, I vow that I will survive and press on. When I can open my right eye, I realize that almost a week has passed since I returned from my fateful holiday. I have not yet received the Cuban declaration papers. I fight off another panic attack. I can barely breathe. My normal composure is now thrown to the wind; my own voice sounds strained beyond recognition as I begin to dial every number given to me by the Peel Regional Police Department.

"Please, I need a restraining order against a Canadian citizen who assaulted me in Cuba."

There's no positive response. My fear has now officially given license to my anger. It pains me even more to have my mother see me like this. I have one more day before my daughter Katrina and Dan return from their holiday in Mexico. What about my other daughter, Daniella, in England?

I've always been a pillar of strength for my family; now, I can't even take my own dog for a walk. It's not that my ego is crushed or my faith in humanity diminished; I simply need the protection of a restraining order to go on with my life.

As fate would have it, early next morning my lawyer calls to inform me that it's time to renew my mortgage. My voice quivers when he asks how my trip to Cuba was.

"Did you get enough sun?" he asks.

"No, Mr. Johansen. I was assaulted in Cuba and I need some advice."

"I'm sorry, did you say 'assaulted?'"

"Yes. My mortgage renewal is the last thing on my mind. I really need to know how I go about obtaining a restraining order."

"There's a chap who's sharing my office. His name is Sheldon Burnstein. He probably knows a lot more than I do. Should I have him call you? Don't worry about the mortgage papers. I'll mail them to you. Just sign them and mail them back to me."

The doorbell rings; it's my neighbour Shelley, again. This time she comes bearing a video.

"How are you feeling, Marisha?" she asks, her children ten paces behind her. "I thought a good video would cheer us all up."

I'm surprised when my mother quickly answers on my behalf.

"That would be great, Shelley."

I want nothing more than to ease my immediate pain. My nerves are so oversensitive that the sound of quiet conversation in my living room bothers me. My favourite songs, melodies, or lyrics, which used to soothe me and energize my spirit, have turned into annoying intrusions. So, I can't comprehend watching a video with my neighbour's children. But I force myself to watch the comedy while Bito lies at my feet. I'm grateful when Shelley sends her teenage daughters home early.

I unfold my woeful tale to Shelley, ending it abruptly. "Look at this list that the police gave to me. I've called this whole page of numbers this week, and I still don't know whether I'm going to obtain the protection of a restraining order."

***

Steve and Liza have already returned. They call to tell me that they have already developed the pictures from Cuba. I didn't realize that they also had photographed the crime scene.

She asks me if I have received the Cuban documents.

"Not yet," I say.

"That's nearly impossible. We have all been pressing Maria to send them to you, as soon as possible."

"Hopefully, I'll get them today."

"When you left, everyone sank into depression. The staff couldn't believe it. The whole resort was in total disbelief. Hell, the locals wanted to take him to the mountains and have him killed. Marisha, I'll call you next week."

I hang up the phone. I stare at the notes, which I have jotted down during our conversation. I add a few more points, and then return to writing in my journal:

January 9, 1999
This morning I have enough courage to look in the
mirror! The swelling is down and the bruising is changing
colours, from black to purple mixed with yellow. My jaw is
still stiff with pain and my lacerated gums still hurt.
Breakfast today, again, is a mashed banana.

I see my mother and Bito hurrying through the front
door. Frost covers the ends of their hair. I know it's
snowing outside, but now I realize it's very cold. My
mother pulls off her hat as the phone rings. Before she can
unbutton her heavy woollen coat, Stephanie from Shoppers
Drug Mart informs me that a fax has arrived for me. My
mother puts her hat back on and trudges through the snow
across to the mall.

A few minutes later we sit beside each other and stare
at the Spanish document. We try to translate it, to no avail.
I tell her that I'll ask my friend Teresa to translate it.

Despite the great care my mother has given me, she
finds that one of my cuts is red and swollen with infection.
The appointment with my longtime family physician is in a
few days. I feel despair and need to see someone to talk to
about it other than my mother. I call the psychologist's
secretary and ask if she can squeeze me in, earlier than my
scheduled appointment for next week, bust she is
unavailable.

***

The counseling session with my psychologist this
afternoon goes extremely quickly. She hears my rap about
the bureaucratic complications and nonsense that daily

stresses me out—mostly sharing with her what has happened in the last few days.

"I have been trying to get the Cuban documentation, and thank God they have faxed it!"

"Marisha that is a tremendous progress!"

The psychologist nods positively and smiles, and in her peaceful way, she asks no more. I continue to update her,

"A friend will translate the Spanish for me."

"It's good that you keep your determination, Marisha," she says, and then continues with the affirmation, which encourages me the most.

"I know that with your intelligence you'll eventually get justice done concerning this crime. What you must concentrate on now is trauma recovery."

Her last statement is agreeable to me because I'm hoping to move on with my life as soon as possible. I leave her office, thanking her for understanding me. I'm feeling great accomplishment, for today!

The following day is particularly cold. I'm still curled up in bed. The sheets are damp from night sweats. I contemplate the items that I'll need for my doctor's appointment. My head feels like a sack of pulp.

I crawl out of the tangled sheets and prepare for the arduous expedition. I dread now leaving the house after my eventful holiday. It will be a laborious undertaking, but the mundane preparation helps me realize that some semblance of reality still exists in my life. I grab a bottle of water and stuff it in my purse. Bito, my dog, thinks he's finally going for a walk with me.

"No, Bito, not today."

There will be other patients in the waiting room, so I need to make myself presentable to the outside world. I search for a scarf to cover my face. My gums sting from the touch of my toothbrush. I try to brush my hair, but it's too painful. The torn, bare spots on my scalp make it impossible. I think about calling Teresa before I leave. I'll need to dress warmly. I notice my teeth are chattering and I'm shivering with the cold, despite having cranked up the thermostat.

I continue to disbelieve my image in the mirror. Will I ever recover? Will I ever feel secure? Since my return from the holiday, my whole behaviour has changed. I have reoccurring fits of anger and weeping.

I have started to resent my mother's kindness. I distance myself from her; I'm insolent and hostile.

"Marisha, are you ready?" she asks.

"Of course, mom!" I reply, and I'm shocked at my unintentional sarcasm.

I watch Bito wagging his tail as he brushes his cuddly body against my legs. I try to pet him, but another flashback enters my mind. Last Christmas, Raffaele and I were in love. What happened to him that night? I can't believe it! I should have never forgiven him after the first incident, that first evening of the holiday. Damn it! I should have never listened to him when he kept begging me for forgiveness. I loved him and I gave him another chance and look what happened. He told me over and over that he loved me that night, just before we went to sleep. One thing I know now is that he lied.

The ringing of the kitchen phone lets me know that I'm still at home.

"Marisha! A man by the name of Sheldon Burnstein wants to talk to you," my mother says from downstairs.

I think it's the civil lawyer, and as I pick up the phone, I feel nervous.

"Hello. This is Marisha Manley."

"Ms. Manley, this is Sheldon Burnstein. Brian Johansen has referred you to me. I hear that you've had an unfortunate incident in Cuba. Is this right?"

"Yes, I was assaulted."

"And now you're having a hard time charging the assault in Canada?"

"That's correct."

"Well, I can start on civil proceedings as soon as you want. I'll need to have the documentation pertaining to the incident."

Realizing that I'm almost late for my doctor's appointment, I ask if I can get in touch with him tomorrow.

A few hours later, the doctor says the only thing that can promote my physical and emotional healing is time. I cling to my mother's arm as I stagger down the hallway after leaving his office. Her strong finger pushes the down button of the elevator. On the way home, I'm thinking that I would heal so much faster if justice would be done!

Finally home! My mailbox is stuffed with thick envelopes.

"It must be the correspondence from Anna Marie and Liza." Mother brings them to me. "Shall I open them for you?"

I don't really want to see the contents of the envelope. Without another word, she places them in her bag and takes Bito for a walk. I go to the kitchen, reheat the soup my mother has prepared, and pour some tea.

The sound of my mother returning with Bito running overexcited through the front door initially irritates me. I reprimand myself for my lack of patience. But then, seeing my mother's rosy cheeks flushed by the brisk wind makes me thankful that she's here with me. I realize I need her so much more now than ever before.

She opens each envelope and sifts through the photos as if shuffling cards, as quickly as she can. My heart trembles. My hands shake; she hands them to me. I browse through the horror story that Steve Joyce documented with photographs.

My caring mother says, "Marisha, Anna Marie's letter documenting the events, combined with the graphic photos of your blood on the bedsheets, floor, and curtains, is enough proof to have this crime resolved."

Anxiety fills me as I view the attack, once again. This time, I see how I looked right after being assaulted: bloodied, terrified, and feeble.

"Mom, this man professed to love me—envisioned a future together with me. How could he savagely beat me like this?"

I cry and she sits in silence, her gentle hands trying to soothe my shaking. I am traumatized, again, as my mind cannot stop racing.

There were no warning signs before Cuba, or were there? Was I so naïve to think that his unexpected violent outburst on the first evening of the holiday was the exception, not the norm? Why did I forgive him? He swore that he'd never hurt me again. He proceeded to show me the same respect and love that I was accustomed to with him before we arrived in Cuba! Love is forgiving. I loved him enough to give him another chance. That love now seems like years away! I snap out of my trance.

"What he did to me is unforgivable." I frown at my mother.

"Marisha, these photos are the evidence of the crime scene. You must have copies made of these, immediately."

She places the photos back into the envelope, stuffs them in her purse, zips it securely, puts on her coat, and then quickly heads across to the mall. I thank the Lord for my mother's strength, again, and for the Canadian vacationers who have helped me so much along the way.

I'm catatonic—frozen by what I have just seen. On one hand, I'm glad the evidence is here, but frightened by the gruesome thought: *It could happen again if I'm unable to obtain justice or at least a restraining order against him.*

Soon my mother returns and sits reading at the dining room table. I try to focus on what's next. I have to return the call from the civil lawyer. I should do that, now. I notice the message machine flashing. Katrina and Dan.

"Mom, can't wait to see you. We'll be back, tonight," Katrina's message says.

My mother and I stare at each other in anguish, sadness in our eyes. I forget to call the civil lawyer and my friend, Ruth; I don't listen to the rest of the messages.

I'm scared and upset; nothing can ease the shock of the mess Dan and Katrina will see when they arrive home.

I'm trying to stay strong for them, but as soon as they enter the house, their shock and disbelief escalate to loud cries and tears. They hold me tightly, without asking for any details or questions.

"How could he do this to you?" Dan cries out.

My mother helps Katrina take her luggage to her room. Everyone remains silent as Katrina unpacks her clothes. I hear Bito barking at the door; Katrina runs to the front door, my mother and I stare at each other with concern.

I hear Ruth. As always, she is punctual. I last saw her before Christmas.

"Katrina? You guys are already back from holiday?" I hear her ask.

"We have just arrived, tonight."

"How was your trip?"

"It was all right, Ruthie," Katrina says as I come downstairs to greet Ruth.

"Oh, my God, Marisha!" Ruth's hands fly up to cover her mouth.

Bito hears her cries and starts to bark. Katrina soothes him as Ruth puts her hand over my shoulder and takes me in her arms. I reluctantly begin once more to tell my horror story.

"I have the Cuban declaration! Ruth, it doesn't mean a damn thing," I tell her.

"Why?"

"Because it happened in Cuba."

"Was he charged in Cuba?"

"Of course! Ruthie, I have declaration papers from the Cuban police confirming that. But it seems that it does not have legal standing in Canada."

"Why not?

"Canada has no jurisdiction to convict a Canadian who commits a crime upon another Canadian in Cuba or in other countries that don't have a treaty with Canada."

"Unbelievable! I've got to check this with the lawyers at my office." She gets up and paces the floor.

"The Cuban police told me that I should return to Canada as soon as possible for the sake of my medical situation, and then charge him here in Canada. I don't know if they purposely misled me to get the case off their hands or if they really didn't know."

"I can't believe that we live in a democratic country and there are no laws to protect us!"

"Ruthie, I will never rest until I receive justice."

The hardest pill to swallow was Raffaele's callous line, "How did God allow this to happen to you." I reiterate his unbelievably harsh words to Ruth.

"How could God allow this to happen to you? What a devil to lay the blame on God. I bet you he knew that there's no law for his crime in Canada. He probably thought he'd get away with this. He's sick."

"This is the only answer I have about why he did this to me."

"But if you had stayed in Cuba, could you have him arrested there?"

"Yes, but in my condition I needed medical attention that could only be provided in Canada."

The phone rings.

"Marisha! It's Cathy. I can't believe what I've heard. You mean to tell me he wasn't arrested at the airport?"

"Cathy, I'm scared! My friend Teresa is getting the declaration papers translated. I hope the charge in Cuba will at least enable me to get a restraining order."

"Marisha, don't forget there are so many people behind you. Even at the resort in Cuba, Laurel told me that he admitted to her he assaulted you. And she's willing to sign an affidavit. Let me know how I can help."

"Let's call Teresa right away," Ruth says as soon as I put down the phone.

I pick up the phone again and dial.

"Marisha, did you get my message?" Teresa asks when we get connected.

"No."

"I'm on my way," she says.

I go upstairs and bring down the file with all the documentation, which my mother has so painstakingly organized. Ruth looks at every paper and is shocked when she peeks at the "holiday" photos.

Teresa arrives. She's dumbfounded when she sees me and tells me how sorry she is that this has happened to me. Then she joins Ruth at the table. They both pour through the photos and once in a while they stare at each other in disbelief.

"I'll get the declaration translated tomorrow. And, I'll make extra copies for you. I should have it ready, in a day or two," Teresa says.

"I'll see what the boys at the firm have to say about it," Ruth says.

They both leave.

That night I fight to fall asleep, but again, I'm interrupted by a call. I reach for it, in a daze, checking the time on the clock radio; who could be calling me at midnight?

"Hello? Hello! Hello! Yes, who is this?"

There's only dead air on the other end of the line. I quickly hang up, my hand shaking. I fumble to dial *69 to find out the call's source. I see that the number matches Raffaele's home phone, so I contact the police.

I force myself to relate my story, once again. These repetitions are hard on my nerves, and I want to scream. The police try to calm me and tell me to dial 911 if he calls again. From downstairs, Katrina and Dan hear me crying.

"Mom! Who was that who called?"

"It was him, except he didn't say a word."

We huddle on the couch in front of the television, but no one is able to watch the movie. I know I'm in for another sleepless night.

Chapter 8. No Criminal Charge, No Compensation!

Morning comes too quickly. It's now eight days since my life, and the life of my family, has so drastically changed. In the morning my mother screens another call.

"It's Crystal and Michael, Marisha. They want to come over."

I must have taken an extra painkiller because I'm more groggy than usual.

"Mom, tell her not during the day since I have to see the psychologist. Better this evening."

I call the crisis unit and make an appointment. Then I search for the civil lawyer's number. A secretary informs me that Mr. Burnstein is at the courthouse today.

"Could you please let him know I called?"

I lie on my bed and think of taking a nap. It's irrelevant if my eyes are open or closed; I can't shake off these panic attacks. Insecure about my safety, I call the contact number for the Justice of the Peace, which the police gave me.

"Please, I need protection," I say, but receive no immediate solution—only more numbers to call.

***

The counseling session with the psychologist today is helping me to deal with the post-trauma a little more. She reminds me that it takes time to recover from such a brutal assault. She listens patiently as I constantly repeat myself.

"My life is completely turned upside down and is taking every ounce out of me. It's depressing with what I have to deal with." I roll my eyes, tears flowing.

"Is the doctor still prescribing antidepressants?"

"Yes, they make me sick," I say. I can hardly control anything in my life anymore. I add, "Julia, by not getting justice, I feel completely helpless."

"We need to focus on your trauma healing, here."

"I know, but each day, seeking justice takes up all of my waking hours."

"Marisha, I know that you must be so drained by all this. I understand that; however, you are the only person who can do this, so you must stay strong."

"I want to heal, but I'm consumed by the phone calls to the Justice of Peace and the retelling of my pain." I pause momentarily, then add, "I'm so busy trying to keep my head above water that I almost forgot about the counseling session with you, today."

She smiles sympathetically and assures me,

"If you ever have to miss a session, please call me, and I will reschedule it for another day." She pauses for awhile, and then in her gentle voice she resumes, "I hope that soon you'll get the peace you need to get back to your life, your profession, as before." She nods bringing a light smile to her face, then continues, "So, has there been any progress in finding protection since the last time we spoke?"

"Well, I've almost exhausted most of the numbers on my calling list for justice. The only contact I have left is a

Justice of the Peace, given to me on my last call today. But I had no time to call since I had to come here."

"Keep it up, Marisha. Don't you give up!" the psychologist encourages me again. Just before I leave, I also let her know that I'm concerned about my daughter Katrina and her boyfriend, Dan. They have returned from their holiday and are devastated by my circumstances.

"Stay strong for them," she says, as if knowing that this is what I have been doing all along for my children.

"I don't want my family hurting!"

"That's understandable. They love you."

I leave feeling relieved because I have vented my frustrations. I know Julia wants to promote my emotional healing, and I believe I am starting to trust her.

Upon my return home, I dial the last number given to me, intending to speak with the Justice of Peace. No chance. I hear only the sound of an answering machine, and it is still business hours.

Frustrated, yet determined to unearth justice, I turn to the page where I stopped writing about the events of my nasty holiday. My mind races faster than I can write. I'll need the information for the civil lawyer. I document today's call log.

Later in the evening, when Crystal and Michael arrive, they share their fury at Raffaele with me. Their anger grows even more: Michael is especially angry at himself because he brought Raffaele into our circle.

"Marisha, if I had not introduced him to you, then this would never have happened!" he keeps saying.

That is true, but I say,

"It's not your fault that he's that way."

Then, Crystal explains that a friend at Osgoode Hall law school is still researching on behalf of my situation and Michael promises to run the case by the lawyer in his office. I hadn't realized how many of my friends are concerned with my case. Their loyalty and help give me hope.

***

It does not take more than a day to learn that the largest legal firms in downtown Toronto have familiarized themselves with my case and have come up empty. The sad reality hits me hard; no recourse exists in my case. No criminal or civil lawyer, no judge, and no part of the legal system can bring this crime into the open, because no statute in Canada covers an assault in Cuba. Everyone is dumbfounded and helpless. My mother can't take it anymore.

"I'll call you, soon," she says. "Keep your faith in the Lord!" She returns to her home. Bito lets out his usual loud proclamations when someone arrives. Now, it is me who peeks to see who it is—my mother is no longer at my home.

Teresa walks in, handing me a large, white envelope. I know what's in it.

"It's late: I have to run. Let me know how you make out with this."

"Thanks again, Teresa."

We used to kiss each other on the cheeks, but now everyone is afraid to. My facial scars are tender. Teresa and

I hug, I feel that awful pain over my face, neck, and shoulders.

The next morning the phone startles me. I don't recognize the number; I pick up anyway, gingerly.

"Hello!"

"Marisha Manley? It's Sheldon Burnstein from Brian Johansen's office. How are you, today?"

I take a deep breath before responding.

"Not too good," I say.

"I'll need to see all of the documentation."

"I have the pages photocopied for you." I'm glad he's willing to take my case, immediately. Then I pause, listening for more encouraging words from him.

"I can't present your case to a judge, as yet."

"Why not, Mr. Burnstein?"

"You must understand that if no charges are laid in the court of Canada, then it will be difficult to proceed with a civil case."

"Oh . . . but, why Mr. Burnstein? I have the Cuban charge translated, evidence in photos of the crime, and witnesses."

"I still can't start proceedings until there's a criminal judgment."

"But, Mr. Burnstein? If he can't be charged in Canada, then how am I going to get any resolution?"

Dan and Katrina are now beside me. Katrina has puffy eyes, and Dan frowns.

"Why don't you bring the documentation at two o'clock on Wednesday, and I'll have a look?" Mr. Burnstein asks.

"I'm sorry, Mr. Burnstein, but I don't feel comfortable in public. Would you be kind enough to come to my house?"

"If that's better for you," he replies.

"Thanks." I sigh with relief. "I'll be at your home at two o'clock on Wednesday afternoon, if that's convenient for you."

"Thanks, again!"

I hang up and make a note concerning the approaching date.

"We were thinking about getting some takeout," Katrina says.

"Honey, I'm sorry, but I'm feeling very dizzy and weak. I have to lie down." The thought of food right now makes me feel queasy.

"You must eat something, Mom, before you go."

Save for a nod, I can't answer her.

I ready myself for counseling at the crisis unit. My concern is what the crisis unit can do for me. I hope they can help me relieve some of my pain. Thank God it's at the hospital, where I don't worry about people seeing my scarred face.

The drive with Katrina is silent; I'm bombarded with physical and mental pain and can't even put on my normal, happy face for my daughter.

I almost lose my composure. I'm at my wit's end when the counselor's shock exceeds mine. My one-hour counseling session deals mostly with her disbelief; she keeps saying,

"I can't believe you cannot charge him."

I leave the crisis unit wondering if I'm wasting my energy and faith, pursuing the elusive grail of justice. I return home and fall into a deep sleep.

Later in the afternoon, Ruth calls to tell me that the most energetic, radical legal students of the most prestigious law school, Osgoode Hall, are shocked to find such a gaping hole in the *Canadian Criminal Code*.

My family and friends are now aware that justice has been denied to me. No one can do anything. All the calls that I've made to the offices of the Justice of the Peace were a waste of time. There's not even the possibility of procuring a restraining order. I feel as if the prison gates have closed on me instead of the criminal.

Flashbacks revisit me in the night. I wake up in cold sweats. I grope for another painkiller and hope for sleep. Then, I hope, in the morning, when I wake up, this will all be over.

Chapter 9. Restraining Order, Please!

I have spent ten long days trying to rationalize how I'm going to charge the assault.

I keep the appointments with Julia at the Yellow Brick House, into whose hands I have entrusted my mental health. Panic attacks that have always occurred at night are beginning to overwhelm me during the day. She says she can see me at two o'clock tomorrow.

My face begins to return to normal, but I cover my scars with ointments. The scars still sting. Getting dressed also remains difficult.

A breath of fresh air! At the clinic, my psychologist walks me through my immediate needs; she listens to my uncontrollable outbursts of anger.

"How could he do this to me? Why? Why? Why? He and I loved each other. Just the day before, he asked me if I would marry him; he said this in front of other people."

She lets me vent. She listens with compassion to my cries.

"How can I live like this? How can I charge him?"

"I know you have great pain, Marisha, but only time can heal it."

I turn away from her, trying to control my tears by staring into the heavy traffic on Yonge Street, trying to lose my pain in the outside, but then I cry out again.

"Julia, I wake up at night, screaming. I'm afraid he's going to kill me. One night last week, I even tore the elastic from my hair, imagining it was his hand."

She hands me another Kleenex and waits for me to compose myself.

"How can I live like this?" I blow my nose. "He's out there. He could still kill me." I clear my throat.

"Marisha, it will take some time. You cannot rush healing."

"But, Julia, I'm petrified! I can't even obtain a restraining order!"

"No doubt, it's very difficult to be in your situation. However, try to stay strong and keep your faith."

I return home from a counseling session slightly less angry. The light on the answering machine is flashing: a call from my mother, another from Crystal, Dana, and Ruth, and an unknown voice—the civil lawyer. I pour some milk and sip it. There is something to reflect on.

***

Now, my counseling is twice a week; I alternate sessions between my psychologist at the Yellow Brick House and the crisis unit at the hospital. The latter evolves into nothing more than shuffling bureaucratic paperwork. The social worker focuses on my inability to charge the crime committed against me and does not offer me counsel with regard to the assault. My anguish certainly does not ease my pain, but I need to restore my mental health. It seems that these sessions at the crisis unit will not be fruitful for me any longer. Perhaps I should not waste her time.

My psychologist Julia, on the other hand, tries her best to help me stay focused on gaining strategies to cope, guiding me to regain my life and faith. However, the counselor at the hospital crisis unit irritates me, enormously. During each session, she constantly repeats, "I can't believe there's no law for your case." These constant comments make me wonder, *who's the therapist here?*

My doctor notes that my facial injuries are finally healing; the swelling has gone down, leaving a bump on the left side of my nose. He takes a few more photographs of my face. He continues to prescribe the antidepressants and the anti-inflammatory pills for my nasal region and back spasms.

"You've got to count your blessings, Marisha," he says, "You could have come home from Cuba in a box."

As much as I am grateful to have survived, I hope to never again have to go through the anguish that I'm forced to deal with every day since that horrible night.

Today after his visit, I drive to the Royal Orchard Plaza; the parking lot is full. I'm tempted to take the designated handicapped space in front of Shoppers Drug Mart. I wait patiently as a young girl takes way too long to back out from her space. I just want to get into the drugstore, fill my prescriptions, and grab some basics at Dominion.

Bags. Heavy bags. Fortunately, one of my students works part-time at Dominion. He graciously puts them in my trunk. Too bad I can't put him in the back seat so he can unload them when I reach home.

My Nissan seems to know its own way home; it shuttles me safely into the driveway. I do my part by pushing the remote; the garage door does its part by opening smoothly. Now, who will magically carry the shopping bags into my kitchen? The cold air hits my injured face as I open the car door. I pop the trunk latch and laboriously carry the first bag of groceries into the house. I rest a bit, and then the other three bags follow the same procedure.

My dog is hungry and needs a walk. Groceries still on the counter, I let him out to relieve himself in the backyard. I'm still afraid to stroll the neighbourhood alone. I start to unpack some groceries, but Bito is protesting at the back door, so I drop everything and let him back in.

"Stop complaining, Bito! I'm hungry, too!" I nose around in the freezer and reach for my favourite comfort food, Haagen-Dazs Cookies & Cream. A plastic bag falls to the floor. Bito sniffs it. Jesus. My hands shake as I realize the ziplock bag contains my dried blood and my hair. I'm feeling nauseous and want to crumble to the floor, but when the phone rings I try to steady myself against the kitchen counter.

"Hello."

"Hey, Marisha, it's me," Monica says. It was her and Sal's kindness that had brought me from the airport to the hospital. Her goodness doesn't stop.

"Hi, Monica." I try my best to respond, but the sound of my voice gives me away.

"Do you want me to call you later?"

"No, Monica. I'm glad you called." My heart is pounding; I need someone to talk to. "Monica! I just found . . . I'm terrified . . . a plastic bag with my bloodied hair and earrings." I begin to sob.

"Marisha, calm down. Remember, your mom put them there to keep as evidence. Oh, by the way, Dana says 'hello' to you. She's been quite sick; she's going through some tests."

"Must be serious."

"I'll let you know as soon as I hear from her. For now, take care of yourself."

I burn lavender candles in my room, then place them at the edge of my bathtub and ease into the steaming warmth, anticipating its proven powers of relief. It feels so good. The calming, aromatic scent teases my sensuality as my body briefly remembers its former pleasures. The water invites my hair, my head, to enter further. However, when the scars on my face touch the water, pleasure turns to pain—a reminder that it has been only twelve days. My doctor was right; it's going to take time. However, I have no time for pleasure. There is a lot of work to be done by this afternoon, and I have to rush. By two o'clock, when my civil lawyer arrives, I have placed all necessary documents on my coffee table for him.

I had assumed that Sheldon Burnstein would be much older. His voice had sounded more mature on the phone. Now before me, in an ill-fitting grey suit, he appears to be fresh out of law school, and a little wet behind the ears. He looks at the folder on the table between us, takes a fast look around the room, and immediately drops his eyes back on my thick file.

"Are these the documents?" he asks.

"Yes, they are."

He takes the evidence in his hands, opens it, and looks at me.

"I need a retainer of one thousand dollars," he says.

I gasp as I take out my chequebook and, casting my last bread on the waters, hope that sooner or later, with a little luck and this lawyer's diligence, I'll receive justice.

"For your protection, you must ask the Justice of the Peace for a peace bond," he says, as I write his name on the cheque.

"Mr. Burnstein," I say.

"Please, it's Sheldon."

"I don't know anymore where I can go." I strain for air.

"Go to the North York Courthouse on Finch and ask for the Justice of the Peace. I'll call you next week," he says, and leaves my home with the photocopied documents in his briefcase.

***

A wonderfully loving family, Sheri and her husband, Dan's parents, offer their support. With an air of confidence, Sheri picks me up at home. She installs me in the passenger seat of her Mercedes and, as if I were her child, secures me by strapping the seat belt across my body. We head off in silence to the office of the Justice of the Peace in the North York area. Today, we are determined to succeed.

The office manager shows us into a room, where she asks us to be seated and closes the door. We wait for the JP. Finally, he steps in.

Immediately, I present him with my evidence—the Cuban declaration and the photos—and I wait patiently. But, like a Chinese gong going off at intervals, again and again, the JP replies,

106

"It's unfortunate that this crime occurred in Cuba. It's outside my jurisdiction. I can't issue you a peace bond."

I reflect on the irony of his title, "Justice of the Peace." Justice of *what* damned peace, if there's no law for my case? It also bothers me enormously that Mr. Burnstein and others, who should know this fact, are all directing me to do the impossible. My confidence is shaken not only by the inequalities of Canadian law, but also by the legal profession.

"What about this Cuban declaration?" I ask him, in what has become chronic irritation. "What about the photos, clear evidence of the crime? Isn't there any law that can be applied?"

There's silence as he plods through the printed documentation.

"No, I can't do anything for you," he says.

I take a deep breath. The JP and Sheri watch for my reaction. My anger erupts; I explode.

"How can I make you understand? I'm afraid for my life."

In silence, he drops the Cuban declaration and turns away. It's clear that he has washed his hands of this pesky case. Flustered, confused, and angry, I pick up my worthless documents and throw them back on the desk, toward him. I cannot believe he's dismissing my case! Sheri and I stand up on opposite sides of his table. He starts walking to the door; Sheri stops him.

"Wait a minute! How is she to live here in the city, without any protection from the attacker? How can she report that this crime has been done to her?"

"I told you, there's nothing I can do."

107

As he moves toward the exit, I'm still hoping that perhaps he'll make an exception and provide me with a peace bond.

"I am Canadian and the offender is Canadian; how can I charge him in Canada?"

For a moment, he stops in silence.

"There's no law for this crime here. There's nothing I can do in your situation. Sorry."

I watch his back as he walks to the door; it shuts, and with it any hope that I've gained something from this day. A feeling of despair and abandonment comes over me—the same one I felt at the airport when the Canadian authorities left me hanging.

I don't want people to stare at my tears and my dark, bruised face; I strain to quickly leave the building of justice. "Building of justice!" What a joke! We hurry down the long hallway and find our way out into the parking lot. I shout like a madwoman into the heavy snowfall.

"He knew he was going to get away with it! He knew that there's no law for this crime!" I cover my face with my hat.

By now, I'm convinced that he knew much more about the law than I did and more than these lawyers seem to know.

"I feel powerless," I say, once we're in the car. Tears run from my eyes.

"Let's not give up yet," Sheri says. "We'll go to another JP tomorrow."

Once again, I'm back at home, alone after another trying day. My well of energy is running dry between my legal pursuits and my twice-weekly counseling sessions.

I'm too physically and emotionally spent to keep my
appointment with Julia. I'll have to wait until next week for
her support.
    I wonder if there's any source of hope for me. So far,
I've exhausted every legal avenue, to no avail. My wheels
are spinning, and when I look back, I'm faced with the
same cold reality.
    The phone rings. It's Cathy, checking up on me.
    I tell her that the same frustrations haunt me, each
day. She relays to me that she feels depressed as she
watches me go through such trying times. She tries to
encourage me.
    "A friend has suggested that you try the Justice of the
Peace office in Newmarket."
    I thank God for her and the other vacationers, who
have given me their unconditional support.
    My civil lawyer, Sheldon Burnstein, tells me, "I can't
possibly file for civil proceedings until Grecci is criminally
charged."
    Another shock for me!
    "I'm upset. How could this happen, Mr. Burnstein?"
    "We have to wait to see what the next Justice of the
Peace will say."
    Even Mr. Burnstein, my civil lawyer, is not able to
proceed. Now, he has the retainer, but for what—if I have
to wait? Wait for what law? I'm determined, at least, to get
the protection of a restraining order. Could there be
another avenue?

Chapter 10. Coincidences, Or...

Overnight, a postcard winter wonderland has suddenly reappeared. The grey slush in my driveway is now covered with a clean, fresh blanket of snow. The fluffy whiteness on the grass and trees in front of my townhouse sparkles beneath the winter's sun.

As inviting as this seems, I still check the weather channel. They report there has been seven centimetres of accumulation. How many inches is that? All I know is that today's road conditions are too hazardous to travel all the way to Newmarket.

Even the phone stays silent. Last night's storm seems to have put everything on hold. The peace bond will have to wait until Monday. I welcome this unexpected rest that Mother Nature has so kindly given me.

Sometimes, in the darkest moments of despair, light miraculously appears from out of nowhere. It's hard to believe in such a coincidence: Late this afternoon, my neighbour, Shelley, calls. She's huffing and puffing on the other end of the line; finally, she catches her breath.

"Marisha, you'd better sit down for this one!"

"What is it?"

"You won't believe this, Marisha! I've just run into Raffaele's ex-wife!"

"What do you mean, Shelley?"

"Listen, I was on the fifth floor of our offices when I heard Gabriella Grecci being paged." Shelley still speaks fast; I'm all ears. I can't believe that this is possible! What is she telling me?

She goes on to explain that she approached Gabriella and asked her if she was related to Raffaele. Gabriella was stunned and immediately asked Shelley how she knew him by the name of "Raffaele" because most people call him "Ralph."

"I tell you, Marisha," Shelley goes on, "this is beyond coincidence!" Shelley stops talking. She takes a deep breath, and then continues. "When I told Gabriella that I know him through you, Marisha, my neighbour, she just about fell over."

"So, what did she say?" I ask.

"Without missing a heartbeat, Gabriella asked, 'Did he do something wrong, again?'"

My stomach churns as Shelley—now totally out of breath—adds to her soap opera scenario.

"Marisha, I told her, 'Yes!' Then, she asked me if it happened in Cuba."

"Shelley, this is completely unreal. I am amazed at how God works in mysterious ways!"

"Marisha, she wants to talk to you right away—after work. Is it all right if I give her your number?"

"Of course."

I start to shiver as I place the phone down. I can't believe this.

As nervous as I am about meeting her, I wonder if Shelley's running into Gabriella is more than mere coincidence. My mind races; I have been anticipating some kind of divine intervention. Perhaps this is a sign.

Within an hour, Gabriella stands at my door. At first glance we are both stunned at how strikingly similar we are physically. We greet one another formally in the hallway.

"This is absolutely incredible, Marisha," Gabriella says.

"I can't believe it," I reply.

We are strangers, but the bizarre circumstances that bring us together create a surreal familiarity, which scares me. Gabriella is the first to speak. She unfolds her story. I can't believe what I am hearing as she shares with me her five years of marriage, mostly with stories of constant escalating abuse.

It blows my mind that only now am I privy to the truth about Raffaele. At first I feel too weak to vent my anger. But as the reality about a man I loved is reflected to me through the face of his former wife, I cannot stay silent. I blurt out my story from the beginning.

Am I not an intelligent woman? Did I temporarily ignore my intuition? I'm angry with myself because I forgave him after his violent outburst on that first evening in Cuba.

"He's on probation for assaulting me and issuing death threats when I was pregnant," Gabriella explains.

This scenario stings my heart and stops my voice. There's nothing left for us to do except cry. I stretch my hands across the table to hold hers. It feels strange to be comforting one another. We are bound only by a crime inflicted upon us by the same person.

"That's not all, Marisha. It gets worst." She lets go of my hand in order to wipe away her tears. "He even beat his sister."

I'm bewildered. Gabriella leans forward on her elbows and stares across the table at me. "His sister confided in me that he slammed her head on a stone floor on her graduation day," she says. Listening to her, I realize that the man is sick. Until now, I had questioned why he'd assaulted me. Now, I know he's truly a monster.

"I can't believe that even his own sister didn't charge him," I say.

"Marisha, that's how they are," Gabriella continues. "There are many skeletons in their family closet, but he is still their son. They hope that the next woman in his life will be the solution. I did not know how violent he could be until I was pregnant."

"And, I saw no warning signs until I was away with him in Cuba."

"He needs to be put away, Marisha. I'm very concerned for Anna's safety," she says, and asks to see the photographs from Cuba.

"You don't think that he would hurt Anna?"

"No, but if he knew that we were talking to each other, he might lose it."

"Can I show the photos to my lawyer?"

"Anything for Anna's safety," I reply and place a thick envelope in her hand.

It's almost 4 A.M. Gabriella and I hug as we say our goodbyes at the front door. As I lay my head on my pillow,

113

I feel thankful, and I drift into sleep while asking God to give me the wisdom and strength to get through next week.

***

Monday morning my knees wobble as I navigate the long hallway of the Newmarket Courthouse. Passing through security, I'm told that the JP's office is at the end of the hallway.

"Slow down, Marisha," I tell myself as pain shoots from my leg to my spine. I almost miss the bullet-proof glass wicket #10, the one I was told to enquire at. The woman behind the partition appears surprisingly friendly.

"How can I help you?" The bright face behind the impersonal divider asks.

"Please, can I see the Justice of the Peace?"

"What is this concerning?"

"I'm here to report a crime committed against me."

She swivels in her seat, opens a large filing cabinet, runs her hand quickly through the files, and pulls out a folder; then, she pushes a piece of paper through the tray.

"Please fill out this form, and I'll see if the JP can see you today."

I write my name next to the heading, *Complainant Information*. I record his name and address under the heading, *Accused Information*, and underneath I give a summary of the assault. I then hand the grey official document back to her. She asks me to take a seat. Knowing that I might be waiting for some time, I go to the restroom. I still have a hard time dealing with anything outside my house.

I'm amazed when I return to the waiting area. The woman behind the wicket calls me. "Ms. Manley, please go to the first door on your right and give this to the secretary." She points in the general direction as she hands back my application.

I open the etched door marked *Justice of the Peace*. In my wildest dreams, I would never have believed that I'd be standing in a courthouse filing an official complaint against my former lover. I enter the narrow hallway and proceed toward the secretary, who sits at a large desk. Without a word, she escorts me through the half-open door to the office of the Justice of the Peace.

A woman with greying blond hair sits behind a heavy cherry wood desk. Her wavy hair is gathered up in a careless bun; her piercing blue eyes are fixed on the document before her. She lifts her head.

"You must be Marisha Manley. I understand you're applying for a peace bond."

"Yes." I answer, and then immediately start explaining my legal dilemma to the JP.

The JP accepts my file. She asks me to provide her with more facts of the assault, as did everyone else. However, I'm not interested in describing the gory elements of the crime again.

"I need protection!" I tell her.

She continues to finger quickly through the photos from Cuba, frowns at them, and then immediately reads the declaration issued by the Cuban authorities. When she comes to the doctor's statement from the Cuban hospital, she shakes her head, and asks me,

"Marisha, are you able to work now?"

"I am a teacher. How can I return to my profession now?

Her countenance is full of compassion, as she continues,

"I used to teach."

Just then, a petite woman with huge brown eyes and black hair steps into the room. Her face looks familiar. I wonder if we might have previously met. The JP introduces her assistant as Michelle Cherney. We shake hands. As she seats herself in the black leather chair beside me, the Justice of the Peace continues.

"Michelle, I'm reviewing Marisha's situation. This is a tough one. She's been brutally assaulted by her ex-boyfriend on holiday in Cuba, where the authorities promised her that she would be able to charge him upon her return to Canada. Upon her arrival in Canada, she tried to charge him. However, she was informed that it was impossible due to a conflict of jurisdiction."

Michelle's cold stare makes me feel very uncomfortable, but her face also bears a hint of empathy. Her forehead is creased, the corners of her mouth droop with sadness. Suddenly, her body moves forward. She points at me.

"Wait a minute. I know you. We work out at the same gym, right?"

The firmness of her voice startles me, but I also place her now.

"My God, I hardly recognize you!" Michelle says, loudly.

Honestly, I'm so tired of these reactions from people. I say, "I am afraid for my life! I need protection from him!"

"Marisha, we'll see what we can do."
I feel relieved. Michelle and the JP both understand me.

"We do care about your safety and well-being," the JP says, and then she assures me, "so, let's see how we can go about getting you protection."

I feel a twinge of renewed confidence—if not in the system, in its people. The encouragement gives me spirit to push my complaint further.

"Can you please check to see if there's anything that can be used here in Canada to charge him for the crime he's committed against me in Cuba?" I ask. The JP hears my desperation, and she assures me,

"We'll do everything possible to help you."
I thank the JP and follow Michelle to the waiting room.

"I hope that there's a way to obtain a peace bond."

Few minutes later, Michelle calls me into her office and tells me,

"Marisha, I've got something here!"

I can't believe it! I can see a lengthy rap sheet—in black and white on the computer screen—the criminal record of the same man who professed his deep love for me. Shivers jolt down my spine. Michelle prints it out, and adds,

"Besides his probation order, there are other run-ins with the law—six all together!"

Despite everything I now know about him, I am still dumbstruck. How could his family deceive me about his character? What devilish ability must a person have to hide his true nature from everyone?

117

"The records show that he has assaulted before. Can you imagine: He has not only assaulted his ex-wife but also others, among them a police officer?" She pauses, and her eyes widen. "His record is certainly a long one. The probation he's currently on is for an assault and a death threat. And, it's still enforceable for another year."

"What can I do to charge him with the crime he's committed against me?" The words rush over my dry tongue.

Michelle appears to search for an answer as she looks down at her desk. Then she looks over at me.

"With his long record, it should be easy to demonstrate to the JP that he's dangerous," she confirms.

"Michelle, I can't thank you enough," I say with gratitude as she gets up and asks me to follow her toward the large office, once again.

The Justice of the Peace is sitting bolt upright in her chair. When she reviews his records, she's determined to help me.

"From what I see in his criminal record, I will act immediately to produce at least some protection for you," she says and makes a notation on my application. She takes another glance at the photos. "With your permission, I'm forwarding these pictures to Detective Eric Strong, to whom I am assigning your case. He's a good man." She pauses and looks at me for a moment. "I hope you can return to your teaching, soon." Then she scribbles down a phone number and hands the paper to me. "Call Detective Strong and set up an appointment with him as soon as possible."

On the way home, I stop for my session with Debra at the crisis unit. The counseling session is a mere recount of what has occurred in the last few days. "You must be exhausted." She sympathizes at first, but keeps shuffling papers. I'm glad that she's not as shocked as she was earlier. "I think that the only way I can get through what is ahead is to go home and get some rest," I explain and look at the door to leave.

I arrive home to find more messages. The light on my answering machine is flickering, madly.

"It's Donovan Vincent from the *Toronto Star* calling for Marisha. Could you please contact me, as soon as possible?"

I return his call immediately.

"Hello, this is Marisha Manley. Mr. Vincent has asked me to get in touch with him. May I speak to him?"

"You certainly may," a pleasant voice, obviously expecting my call, replies. "Let me connect you to him."

I hear a click, followed by a very energetic male voice that sounds to me like one of my twelfth-grade students.

"Hello, Marisha. I heard you're having a difficult time charging a crime that happened to you in Cuba. Am I correct?"

"Yes, it's been a nightmare."

"Our newspaper is interested in reporting your case; it is rare and warrants appropriate justice."

I listen carefully to his every word, concluding that the media may be the best way to get my legal problems noticed and solved, and the reporter persuades me to see him.

Chapter 11. Detective Strong takes Charge

Today, Katrina takes time off work to accompany me to York Regional Police headquarters in Richmond Hill. My briefcase has the peace bond application on which the JP has written:

ASSAULT—MAN ON PROBATION—WHERE? CAN HE BE HAD FOR A BREACH?

"May I help you?" the police officer behind the counter asks.

"I'm here to see Detective Strong," I reply.

"You must be Marisha Manley," a bold voice cuts through the front reception area. A tall, imposing, well-dressed man walks briskly toward us and offers his large hand.

"A pleasure to meet you, Ms. Manley! I'm Detective Eric Strong." After shaking hands, he turns toward Katrina. "And, who might this young lady be?"

"This is my daughter, Katrina."

"Glad to meet you, Katrina."

As soon as we sit down in his cubicle, I hand him the application for the peace bond and begin explaining my dilemma.

"Detective Strong, there is no law in Canada that enables me to charge him with the assault."

"This is a serious matter," he replies, and then pauses. "I agree; anyone so violent must be put away."

"Detective Strong?" Katrina says, as if she's asking for permission to speak. Her body twists from side to side, squirming around in her chair. "Someone told me just the other day they heard in the news about two Canadian businessmen on holiday in Haiti; one of them was assaulted by the other. Now, the victim has returned to Canada and he cannot charge the offender. My mother is not the only case. There must be many others. How can there be no law?" She stops, but her hands twirl frantically.

Across the desk, Strong appears fatherly.

"It's horrible, I agree. Let's see what I can do. I'll need to ask you some questions."

"Sure, Detective Strong," I answer, and immediately ask, "Can Katrina wait for me outside?"

"Certainly." He looks toward her and smiles. "Katrina, make yourself at home. There's coffee and doughnuts in the cafeteria, third door on your left."

"Thanks," she replies and leaves the tiny office.

Detective Strong proceeds to ask me questions and meticulously jots down my answers. I am more at ease when he starts addressing me by my first name.

"Marisha, I understand you're a teacher. I'm sure you'll find it easy to understand the law."

I'm encouraged by his personal attention.

"In your unusual case, it's important for you to know where you stand within the parameters of the law."

The words, "unusual case" makes me feel apprehensive, as he continues.

"I'll do my best to see that he does not go unpunished; this crime is grave and he's a danger to society as a whole."

He then opens his drawer and reaches for a book; it resembles a high school text, the cover bears the words in bold print, *THE CRIMINAL CODE OF CANADA.*

"I will read to you *Criminal Code 268, Section 1.*" He pauses and shows me a section in the book in bold print.

"UNLAWFULLY CAUSING BODILY HARM— AGGRAVATED ASSAULT"

He stops and looks up at me and explains,

'Every one commits an aggravated assault who wounds, maims, disfigures or endangers the life of the complainant.'"

He pauses, and then flips to the next page of the book, and continues,

"Let's look now at the *Code 268, Section 2* and see what it says about the punishment for this crime... 'Every one who unlawfully causes bodily harm to any person is guilty of an indictable offence and liable to imprisonment for a term not exceeding fourteen years.'" He stops. "You must understand that this is what he would have been charged with had he committed this kind of an assault in Canada."

He pauses again, and looks at me. I'm silenced; my grief that I can't charge my perpetrator with this law only aggravates me.

"He has committed a very serious crime," Detective Strong says.

"Yes. Any more blows to my head and I would surely be dead." I almost start to cry.

He stares at the photos taken by Steve Joyce.

"Looking at the scene of the crime, it's a miracle that you escaped from the attack. There's another important reality here. You need to know that by assaulting, your attacker has committed a crime upon a crime."

He seems deep in thought.

"What does this mean, Detective Strong?" I ask.

He slowly tilts his head forward and looks straight at me.

"Under *Section 1* of *Criminal Code 733.1*, he has also breached his probation order. This means that because he has committed another crime when he was under oath to keep the peace and be of good behaviour, he has actually breached his probation order."

"Then, there's something in the law that could apply in my case, here in Canada?" I ask with enthusiasm.

"His probation order is still active. He is still bound by the terms of that order, which clearly stipulate that he is to observe the law and be of good behaviour."

"Do you mean that he can be charged for the assault he committed upon me?"

Strong analyses,

"We'll see," he says. "After I complete an investigation, I will take your case to the Crown counsel's office." He pauses and then looks at me sternly for a moment. "I must insist that you have patience while this investigation is underway."

"Sure," I nod. "If it's okay with you, I would like to have my daughter hear this."

Strong calls Katrina in. I smile at her when she walks in.

"Detective Strong will conduct an investigation. Katrina, there's a good chance he'll be charged!" I say. I can feel the energy, and even some hope, returning. "I'll do my best. But first, you need protection." He smiles, assuring Katrina and me. He picks up my peace bond application, looks at the document again, and then at me. *"Now, let me read to you from Criminal Code 810, Subsection 1."* He pauses. "I hope you will understand that I do want to protect you from this vicious person. The extent of this assault looks like an attempted murder."

He picks up *The Criminal Code of Canada once again*, opens it, and begins to read:

"Information may be laid before a justice by or on behalf of any person who fears on reasonable grounds that another person will cause personal injury to him or her." Strong stops here for a moment, then speaking more slowly, he continues. "I will enforce a twelve months peace bond —a restraining order keeping him from coming close to you, your family, or your friends. I will red dot your dwelling to protect your home from him. This will be effective as of today."

I am overcome with gratitude. Finally, something is being done to save me from further harm. He half smiles, then picks up my Cuban declaration papers from the stack of documentation. He studies every page more closely. When he's finished reading he looks up.

"The physical evidence of your injuries is not enough," he says. He seems to be deep in thought for awhile; then, he lifts his eyes and continues.

"We'll need witnesses—someone who could place him at the scene of the crime or anyone hearing him admit his guilt."

I take a deep breath.

"Of course, Laurel. Laurel at the resort. She's perfect," I say as I clasp my hands together and look toward heaven. "Detective Strong, she's one of the Canadian vacationers who confronted him at the resort. When she asked him, 'How could you do this to Marisha?' he responded that it was the first time he had ever hit a woman."

Detective Strong is scribbling notes.

"You're lucky." He nods. "Can we get her to sign an affidavit?"

"Yes, her note is somewhere here in the plastic bag," I say, pointing to the documentation. Detective Strong moves the file toward me. I flip eagerly through the bundle of papers.

"Her statement about admitting to the assault is important," he says.

"Here it is, Detective Strong." I pull out a pink note from a shiny clear plastic envelope. I hand it to him. The paper appears as if it has gone through a washing machine.

"Look, here's her home number."

"Are these also the contact numbers from the other vacationers?" he asks, as he looks at the envelope.

"Yes and here's even more. These people gave their numbers to Cathy during the flight home. They have also mentioned that they're willing to be witnesses."

"Great. However, Marisha, we first need to record a video deposition. It will be your personal statement to present to the Justice of the Peace."

"You mean, you will tape the interview on camera?"

"Yes, to record the details of your association with Raffaele and to make a record of your current injuries. Would you be able to do that, this week?"

"Of course."

"Please help us, Detective Strong," Katrina says.

"I'll do my best. However, we must be diligent. The deposition is the first step. Friday at one o'clock okay with you?"

"Sure, that's fine."

"I warn you, a video deposition can be very draining. It's advisable for you to bring someone with you."

Katrina drops me at home and goes back to her office. I check my messages and return the most important one to my lawyer. He tells me that the bank has agreed to add another $10,000 to my existing mortgage. I'm happy for the breathing room, but my house is my only financial security. What else can I do? I need money to survive.

The injuries have surfaced again. This time it's a stabbing neck ache. I'm forced to lie down on the couch more often. When I awake, Katrina and Dan call me. Dan has moved in with us now; it seems to be the best solution. I'm more than grateful for their presence, as I still labour under the fear that my attacker may return.

Another sleepless night occurs. As hard as I try, I cannot block out the vivid images. My mind races. The first call of the morning is a welcome return to reality. I pick it up with a weak, "Hello."

"Is this Marisha Manley?" The caller introduces herself as Alice Rondal. I think to myself, *I have never had so many strangers calling me.*

"What is your name, again? Can you please spell it for me?"

"It's Rondal, R...o... n... d... a...l. Detective Strong asked me to contact you. I understand you're going through quite a legal battle. I work for the Yellow Brick House in Aurora. We are a charitable organization assisting people with counseling and legal services."

"My family doctor already referred me to the Yellow Brick House in Thornhill. I'm seeing my psychologist, Julia, there."

"Your doctor has steered you in the right direction. I know Julia. She's a great counselor. I just want to touch base with you and let you know that I'm available anytime. I know how hard it must be for you to be unable to charge him with the assault."

"I never thought I would be going through anything like this."

"I'm sure we'll get him, and when we do it will be my pleasure to be there to assist you during court appearances."

"Thank you. I appreciate this, Alice."

"No thanks required. It's my job. We also have a lawyer, Sheila, who can help you with any legal questions you might have. If you wish, I could put you in touch with her."

"That's very kind of you, but I wish my case was that simple."

As much as I don't want to complain continually, I can't stop myself from voicing my pain.

"There's no jurisdiction to charge him here in Canada. The only hope I have right now is Detective Strong."

"Somehow he has to be stopped before he hurts anyone else," she says.

The cold seems to penetrate me more now. I dress warmly; extra sweaters and jackets are now the norm. I feel 20 years older. I hope that today I'll not break down during my counseling session. I hate being this weak.

***

I drive back home as fast as I can. Fear and anxiety make me push the automatic door opener from halfway down the block and slide the car quickly into the security of my garage. The cold, brisk air stings me more than usual today. I fumble with my house keys in a rush to get inside.

I want to hide under my warm blankets, but I must respond to the two messages left on my answering machine. The first is from Detective Strong.

"Marisha, I spoke to his probation officer this morning. She's calling him in for an interview. She's going to show him the photos. I made an appointment for you to see the JP, Hazel Walker, about the peace bond." He clears his throat and then continues. "I also contacted Gabriella and explained to her that I'm handling the investigation; I've asked her not to call his probation officer as it might jeopardize the case."

I slide into bed and pull the comforter up to my chin in hope that the phone doesn't ring too soon. But it does. After what seems like only minutes of sleep, I notice that it's dark outside. Who could be calling me at this hour?

129

It's Gabriella. The clock shows ten to five.

"Marisha, I'm just getting off work. Is it all right if I drop by? We really have to talk."

"What about, Gabriella?"

"My lawyer said that we must write a letter to his probation officer. She must be informed about what he has done to you," she says.

"Gabriella, Detective Strong is already taking care of that."

"But, Marisha, I don't want him to see Anna. Who knows how crazy he will get."

As much as I want him to be punished, I choose to stick with Detective Strong's investigation.

"Gabriella, I understand your concern for Anna's safety, but Strong has just left me a message emphatically requesting that we wait."

"Marisha, I don't want Anna visiting him, anymore."

"Gabriella, it's crucial that we both cooperate with law enforcement. Otherwise, if he finds out that we're both connected to this case, he might leave the country."

"Aren't you angry about what he did to you?" she asks.

"Gabriella, I think it's best that we stay calm. Let's wait. I'll call you as soon as I hear from Detective Strong."

I feel for her, but at the same time my logic tells me not to get caught up in her anger and instead wait for justice to take its course.

Later in the day my thoughtful neighbour, Shelley, arrives at my door. She is carrying an aromatherapy kit, eager to apply scented oils to my temples, shoulders, and neck.

"Breathe deep," she says, and places a drop of the wonderful aroma on my forehead. "This will help you relax." She smiles. The lovely scent of lavender immediately calms me. It has always been my favourite fragrance. Thanks, Shelley. Tonight, I'm tranquil and more than grateful for a full night's sleep.

During the next counseling session with the psychologist, I breathe a bit lighter. I explain, "I wake up in a more positive mood. So far, the last few days appear destined to bring goodness. Now, instead of the glass appearing half empty, it is half full—thanks to JP Hazel Walker, who has assigned Detective Strong to my case. This Friday, I have to be at the Newmarket Courthouse for a deposition."

"You'll need to gather all your strength for the deposition," she states and gives me a warm smile. She then says, "I'm glad that you're not giving up. Remember, getting justice is a big part of your healing."

I can't help telling her more of the good news.

"Laurel, who witnessed him saying to the Cuban police that he assaulted me, has been contacted. Detective Strong has spoken with her about an affidavit."

"That's wonderful, Marisha!" she cheers me on, and I continue.

"She told me that she's going back to Ottawa to article in a firm, specializing in war crime tribunals. However, she assured me that she is more than willing to swear an affidavit. She gave me her cell number and agreed that she'll do everything to get him charged. She even said that she knows that Raffaele was lying when he claimed that a local had assaulted me. Laurel said that a group of tourists had been talking about what had happened to me the night before. When Raffaele overheard the conversation, he approached the group, demanding that they not talk behind his back. Laurel confronted him by saying, 'What do you expect when you beat an innocent woman half to death?' He had stood there, dumbfounded, and then had had the nerve to say, 'This is the first time I ever hit a woman.' I later discovered that he also beat up his pregnant ex-wife."

"It just shows how cowardly he is," the psychologist affirms.

"It shows me how dangerous he is!" I reply and then add,

"Laurel said that they couldn't believe he had no feelings for my suffering or showed any sign of remorse. When they saw him during breakfast, the way he was smiling made her feel nauseous." I begin to cry.

"Marisha, he's a sick man. He cannot love anyone, not even himself." The psychologist's words are the truth. I know that I must face reality: He never loved me!"

Chapter 12. Police and Newspapers Interviews

This Friday is another nippy morning. My warm breath seeps from underneath my scarf to fog my sunglasses. The wind swirls the fluffy white powder as it gathers on the hardened piles of grey snow.

I buzz Sheri's doorbell. We climb into her car and drive slowly north to the police station. After a warm greeting, Detective Strong ushers us into a very small room where he offers coffee, water or a soft drink. He designates the seating arrangements.

"I'll be conducting a question and answer interview. When I ask you a question, please respond to it immediately," he says. His eyes turn toward the right corner of the room. Sheri and I follow his every move as he points to a small-screened window.

"Please make sure you look directly at the camera located there." He turns to us,

"If we run out of tape, a red light will appear above the window. And, Marisha, if it becomes difficult at any time, we'll stop and take a break. Is that okay with you?"

"Yes." Sheri and I both nod.

He motions with his hand toward the camera room; immediately, a green light shows up. We all look directly at the camera window.

D.S. *My name is Detective Eric Strong, badge number 299, from the York Regional Police. On my right is Marisha Manley. Would you introduce yourself, please?*
M.M. *My name is Marisha Manley.*
D.S. *Please give your address and date of birth.*
After I provide the details of my identity, he then turns to Sheri.
D.S. *And, with Marisha, here, today is her friend. Would you introduce yourself, please?*
S.M. *My name is Sheri Menot.*
D.S. *Would you mind giving us your address, please?*
She provides it.
D.S. *And, what is your relationship to Marisha?*
S.M. *First of all, we are good friends, and her daughter and my son are girlfriend and boyfriend.*
Detective Strong makes a note and directs the next question to me.
D.S. *I'm going to start reading to you, Marisha. Do you understand that what is being said in this room is now being videotaped?*
M.M. *Yes, I do.*
D.S. *I'm Officer Detective Eric Strong, badge number 299, from the York Regional Police and present with us is Sheri Menot. I mark this statement as Document Number 25, given on Friday, the 15th day of January 1999, and the time is 12:54 P.M. We are videotaping at Number 2 District, town of Richmond Hill, in the Region of York. I'm going to leave the room, momentarily, to bring in a commissioner, who will administer the oath to you, Marisha.*

Immediately, a middle-aged well-groomed lady with short blond hair enters the room; Detective Strong introduces us officially on camera.

D.S. *Marisha Manley, this is Rose McCullen, and this is Sheri Menot, a friend of Marisha.*

The commissioner sits down.

R.M. *Please take the Bible in your right hand. Do you, Marisha Manley, swear that the evidence you shall give will be the truth, the whole truth, and nothing but the truth?*

M.M. *Yes, I do.*

I look straight toward the lens.

Detective Strong returns; without wasting time, he goes immediately into the official interview.

D.S. *Marisha Manley, is this true that you are willing to provide us a statement concerning this investigation of an assault on January 2, 1999?*

M.M. *I agree that it is an assault, but it's more than an assault! It's . . .*

My breathing becomes noticeably heavy; I pause to gain enough strength to tell my story again.

At this point, I don't know if it was premeditated. I was almost killed!

D.S. *Okay?*

Detective Strong gently urges me to answer the question that was asked, but I still blurt out my pain.

M.M. *I almost died.*

D.S. *But that's correct—that you have expressed your willingness to provide us a statement concerning the investigation of an assault?*

M.M. *Definitely, yes.*

D.S. *You may be a witness in court, concerning the events you're about to provide in this statement. If at any time you change your statement or claim not to remember the events, the contents of this video statement may be used in evidence in court. Do you understand?*
M.M. *Yes, I do!*
The word "court" already frightens me. I have never even attended court proceedings, let alone been a participant in one.
D.S. *Would you testify truthfully in court proceedings, involving any person charged as a result of this investigation?*
His question lingers in my mind. He repeats it. Finally, I answer it.
M.M. *Yes.*
D.S. *I want you to understand clearly that you do not have to speak to the police, and that anything that you say may be used in court.* He pauses. *Do you understand?*
M.M. *Yes, I do.*
D.S. *If you're spoken to by a police officer or person of authority in connection with this investigation, I want it clearly understood that I do not want to influence you in making a statement. Do you understand?*
M.M. *Yes, I do.*
D.S. *I want you to clearly understand that it's a criminal offence to wilfully obstruct or mislead a police officer who is conducting an investigation, and knowingly to make a false statement of your oath is a crime. Do you understand?*
M.M. *Yes.*

Already exhausted, my hand on my chest and my head bowed, I cannot restrain myself from voicing my anger that there's no law for me to charge. Before I can raise my head again, I utter some heated words and sob. Strong hands me a Kleenex.

"Let's just stick to the incident that happened to you!"

"I'll try."

"Do you want clarification of anything that I have said to you so far?"

"No, I understood everything." I wipe my nose. My head is beginning to throb.

"Do you have any questions?"

"No, I don't."

I keep wiping my nose. I feel overheated; I wish I could take off my jacket.

"Okay," he nods. "Can you read this over?"

"Yes."

"I'm going to quote all of your answers to make sure that they are totally correct."

"Sure," I respond.

I watch him as he flips through paperwork. He straightens himself up in his chair and resumes the interview.

"Let's start at the top," he says and hands me the top sheet.

I scan the official witness statement, noticing my handwritten name filling in all of the blanks. I recite every single word of the document and initial it each time my name appears. Then, we resume the videotaped interview.

D.S. *Marisha, yesterday afternoon you came to the front desk of the York Regional Police headquarters and you were talking to a uniformed police officer before I met you. Correct? And, soon after that, you relayed to me a situation that you were involved in on your vacation in Cuba. Can you tell me what happened? First of all, why were you in Cuba?*

M.M. *It was a Christmas gift from my boyfriend. He purchased an all-inclusive trip for us two to a resort to Cuba.* I think to myself; what a sick joke for a gift! Gift from hell!

D.S. *Tell us what happened prior to Cuba.*

M.M. *Just before we left for Cuba, everything was fine. Our families were at each other's homes celebrating Christmas. On Friday, we were at his parents', Saturday at his sister's, and on Christmas Day we all gathered at my home. I still can't believe what he did to me.*

I start to cry. My whole body shakes. Sheri puts her hand on mine to comfort me. I compose myself and continue.

Prior to Cuba, we were constantly together for six months. There was no indication that he was abusive in any way. On the contrary, he loved me—was kind and gentle toward me. During those six months, we also brought one another's families into our relationship. His parents had me over for Sunday dinners and vice versa. I only remember him raising his voice once. I heard him shouting in Italian, something at his parents' house, when I was standing at the front door.

I pause. As much as I try to remain objective, I just can't help myself from adding my feeling to my testimony. It just pours out.

M.M. *It was not just an assault. One punch is an assault. He beat me so viciously that if I hadn't escaped he could have killed me. A few more blows to my head and I surely would have been dead in that hotel room in Cuba. I cannot charge him here for attempted murder because there's no law for it. The room was covered with blood everywhere, on the bed, on the floor and on his hands.*

Detective Strong stops writing as I rant on.

M.M. *I don't know what is going to happen to me. There must be justice. I'm not looking for revenge. If I was, I would have gone to see his parents and shown them the pictures of what he did to me.*

Detective Strong remains patient, still bent over the stack of paperwork.

D.S. *Marisha, let's clarify a few things before we go on. Who's Raffaele Grecci?*

M.M. *Raffaele Grecci is my former boyfriend, who assaulted me in Cuba. I first knew him as 'Ralph.'*

D.S. *How and when did you first meet Raffaele Grecci?*

M.M. *I met Raffaele Grecci at the end of last June, through friends.*

D.S. *How would you describe your relationship with him?*

M.M. *We were a very loving couple from the time we met. In the first two months we were just friends, and then the friendship evolved into a much deeper relationship. We had picnics together. Our families were meshing. We even*

started to attend church on Sundays. We were planning to have a life, together; he even proposed marriage to me in front of Liza and Steve, a couple we met in Cuba, two days before he attacked me. I can't comprehend why he suddenly wanted to kill me. It's a nightmare.
I break down, again. Detective Strong motions to the camera to stop the taping. He suggests that we take a break, have coffee and a doughnut, and then resume ten minutes later. Perfect timing: My mouth is dry; my voice is becoming hoarse.
I sit silently sipping my coffee as Sheri offers more words of encouragement. The ten-minute break flies by. Detective Strong leans on the doorway of the cafeteria.
"Are you ready to continue?" he asks
"I'll try my best."
M.M. *As I said before* (I turn my head toward the camera) *our families were getting along; everyone was happy that we were together. There was no sign that he had a violent nature.* I fight to contain my anger, but it erupts again. *I don't understand why he attacked out of the blue, that night. In my wildest dream I could never believe that he was capable of such an act.*
Detective Strong gently urges me to answer the questions directly.
D.S. *Can you describe your holiday in Cuba prior to the attack?*
M.M. *On our first night in Cuba, he began to act aggressively toward me. While we were sitting at a table watching the musical review, for some reason he accused me in front of the other people at our table of looking at another man. I was shocked. I got scared of him. I asked*

him, "Why would you think that way?" I tried to reassure him, but he only became angrier. He started calling me terrible names. At that point, I got up from the table and left, crying all the way to the suite. A few minutes later, after washing the tears from my face, he walked in, yelling more obscenities. He approached me and hit me with his arm so hard that I fell to the stone floor; then he left the room. I got up and hurried to the front desk, where I asked the attendant to please give me another room.

I pause and blow my nose.

M.M. *I reported the incident to the resort's management. I begged them to get me on the next flight home. Hours later, the manager and the tour guide explained to me that there was no possibility of any flights until the following week. They provided me with my own suite at the other end of the resort, far away from Raffaele Grecci. The following day, the tour guide took me to the resort doctor to be treated for an injury. I had such a bad bruise on my leg; I wrapped a long skirt around me to cover it up. I was limping. A few ladies I met the night before asked me why I was limping.*

I stop to take a sip of water, clear my voice, and then I continue.

M.M. *During the next few days, Raffaele Grecci constantly approached me, asking for forgiveness. I couldn't. I only kept asking him why he hit me. He didn't have an answer. He just kept telling me that he loved me and that if I took him back he would never get angry. This went on for three days. He even agreed to attend anger management counseling when he returned to Canada. I kept my distance from him.*

This further telling of the graphic details weakens my condition. Exhausted, I still continue.

M.M. *The first day we actually spent together was on a trip to Santiago with a group of other vacationers from the resort. I was not about to move back into the same room with him, at this point, even though he treated me extremely well that day. After a few days of heart-to-heart talks, I was beginning to trust him again. Then, on the 31st of December, just before the New Year's party, without my permission, Raffaele Grecci had a porter bring his bags to my room. He stood at the door, begging me to let him stay, with a firm promise that he would behave. At that moment, I felt compassion for him, forgave him, and let him in.*

D.S. *It's obvious that he did not keep his promise.*

M.M. *No, he did not.* I nod. My eyes fill with tears.

D.S. *Can you continue, Marisha? Please tell us what happened that evening.*

I wipe my eyes, and resume.

M.M. *It was the last day of the holiday. We had supper with another group of Canadian vacationers. Afterward, we went to watch the performance. Before retiring, many of us gathered on the patio near the beach. During that time, we laughed, danced, and enjoyed recapping each other's holiday stories, and with those that had become friends, we exchanged farewells and addresses. It was about 1 A.M. We said our final good nights, and we headed for my suite, arm in arm. I remember feeling romantic toward Raffaele Grecci, at that point; I smiled and looked at him. He put his arms around me and kissed me.*

I need to catch my breath; I pause for a moment. Sheri reaches toward me and wraps my hands in hers.

"Keep going—you're doing well. It's okay," she says.

I take another sip of water and slowly recover my ability to speak.

M.M. *But then, as soon as we were inside my suite, the atmosphere changed. He told me something about Anna Marie's husband having told him that I had hugged him inappropriately. I was very surprised because I didn't understand where this was coming from; I told him it wasn't true and I went on to tell Raffaele that if Anna Marie's husband felt that I had offended him in any way, I must speak to both of them, at once. I left for their room with Raffaele following me down the stairway. After a few knocks on their door, Anna Marie opened the door. I apologized to them for the late visit and went on to explain my reason why I was there. I asked Mike if he had told Raffaele that I had hugged him inappropriately. Mike and Anna Marie were very surprised and Mike immediately answered, "Absolutely not and I never said anything like that to Raffaele."*

Pain overtakes me. I pause for a moment. It's getting more difficult for me to talk about the events of that horrible night.

M.M. *Then there was a very quiet moment in the room. Anna Marie and Mike were standing stunned and I was disconcerted. I turned to Raffaele and looked at him. He said nothing. He just stretched out his arms and walked toward me, hugged me, and, at the same time, apologized to Mike and Anna Marie. Then we left their room. There* *was silence between Raffaele and me as we were returning to my suite.*

I just keep testifying on camera, but inside I'm trying to block out the horrible images, which race in my mind. I hope for strength to get through this deposition. I resume.

M.M. *I felt very upset that Raffaele had created such an unpleasant incident. He'd lied to me and made Anna Marie and Mike upset, but I did not make a big issue of it, thinking it was better to leave it alone. I just wanted to go to sleep, so once we were inside my suite, I said to Raffaele that it would be only a few hours before we would need to be up, packed, and ready to leave for the airport. So we'd better get to sleep.*

I concentrate and try not to take my eyes off the camera as I reach for the glass of water, take a sip, clear my throat, and then resume speaking.

M.M. *I readied myself for bed and laid down. Raffaele was still having his last cigarette out on the balcony when I fell asleep. The next thing I remember, I woke up, barely conscious, in a state of shock. I was terrified; I was being brutally beaten.* My voice gets hoarse, but I speak even faster now. I just want to get through the testimony as soon as possible. *The pain was excruciating; my head and my face were throbbing. I was held by my hair and punched in my face and head. I felt more and more pain with each blow to my body. I was face down on the bed. My head kept swinging back and forth from each blow of his fist. I could not gain enough strength to scream. I felt blood squirting out of my face unto the pillow. With all my might, I tried to tear myself away from* *him, but Raffaele held me by my hair, punched me, and kept yelling, "I will kill you! I will kill you! I will kill you!"*

My heart is pounding so hard that it feels as if it will explode. I clear my throat and take another sip of water.

M.M. *I screamed continuously, "Please let me go!" But he did not stop holding me down and hitting me. I kept trying to push him off me, but he became even more violent and I couldn't get free. I felt that I was dying. I felt blood pouring from my body as he continued to hit my head and face. I kept screaming, "'Why are you doing this to me? Please let me go!"*

He just kept beating me.

I feel like I'm going to be sick, but I rush to tell the end of the gruesome events.

M.M. *I don't know how I managed to pull myself away from him. Somehow I yanked my hair from his hand and forced him off my back. I remember seeing my blood on the floor as I slid off the bed. I picked up a robe, covered myself with it, and ran as fast I could for the exit. Behind me, I could hear Raffaele say, "Now, I'm going to jail, for sure" as he pursued me.*

Down the stairs I ran, screaming, "Help me! Please, someone help me!"

My body is shaking; I'm short of breath, but I continue.

M.M. *I knocked on every door that I passed. A door opened. Luckily, it was Liza and her husband. Immediately, they took me inside. Liza walked me to the bathroom. She was trying to have me wash the blood off in the sink. However, when I looked into the mirror and saw myself, I passed out.*

Only the sound of weeping is heard in the room. The tears, which I had tried to hold back, now pour like rain from my eyes, stinging my scarred face. Sheri gives me a Kleenex.

D.S. *What time would have this occurred?*

I respond with my last energy.

M.M. *It happened somewhere between one and two o'clock in the morning.*

D.S. *So, the injuries we see on your face right now, the cuts, the bruising, and the swollen eye, are the result of this attack?*

M.M. *Yes.*

Detective Strong raises his hand in front of the camera window.

D.S. *We'll stop here.*

I'm relieved that the deposition is over. From the minute the tape began to roll till now, the three and a half hours seem endless. I have done this again and again—with family, with friends, with detectives, with lawyers, and counselors. I feel as though I am hurling through a horrific twilight zone. I'm tired, but force myself to hear what Detective Strong has to say.

"I will deliver this video statement, your Cuban declaration, and his breach of probation to his probation officer, in person," he says. "I'll ask her to get in touch with the Justice of the Peace in Newmarket. And, hopefully, they'll issue a temporary restraining order."

I'm glad to have Detective Strong assigned to my case.

"I'll be contacting the Canadian Embassy to see if the charge in Cuba can be transferred to Canada." He smiles.

"Thank you, Detective Strong."

"Don't even mention it."

I feel worn out emotionally and physically, but I'm satisfied that the wheels of justice are beginning to move.

"I hope this video statement will bring my case into the open," I say.

"The police shouldn't let him get away with the crime," Sheri replies.

In silence, each deep in her own thoughts, we drive to Sheri's home. I drop her off.

"I don't know what I would do if I didn't have family around me," I say.

"Marisha, we'll always be here for each other," she replies.

"Gabriella is coming for a visit tonight at six. She's bringing Anna, so I'll take a rest before they arrive," I say.

"Definitely, take a rest, Marisha. Let me know what she says."

It is easier said than done. I wait for them until six, and then much later; no one appears at my doorstep. I wonder why they are so late, worried and a bit concerned because it is now starting to snow heavily outside.

Finally, the doorbell rings twice. I hear Anna pounding, just as she used to do. When I open the door, Anna looks up at me shyly; her arms are wrapped around her mother's knees. I see Gabriella's face, whiter than the snow, and her expression is one of nervous pain. I feel uneasy, too, because this is the first time I have seen Anna without her father.

"Marisha?" Anna fixes her bright eyes on me. I smile and I fight at the same to contain my emotion. Gabriella

147

announces, "Sorry I'm late, but I had a confrontation with Raffaele."

"I'm glad both of you are here," I say as I hang up their coats and smile at Anna.

"Hi sweetie!" I say. She gazes at me shyly now and then looks toward her mom, Gabriella.

"Do you want to pet Bito?" I ask and reach for her little hand. She giggles, as usual, jumps a bit, and then yells, "Bito, Bito," and runs off with him to the living room. I look at Gabriella; she begins to talk and we walk toward the living room.

"Marisha, tonight he showed up earlier at my door, demanding to see Anna. I refused." Gabriella's voice gets louder with ever word, "He protested, so I had to call the police."

"So what did they say?" My eyes are still on Gabriella.

"They told me he had the right to see his daughter on his visitation days. So I told them what he did to you. Raffaele was so shocked that I knew about it; he exploded and immediately left." She sits down but I am still standing. I ask,

"Have you contacted your lawyer?"

"Yes. But I can't do anything until the probation officer interviews Raffaele." Gabriella frowns. "I hope when she hears what he has done to you, it will reinforce my situation with Anna."

"Let me get some crayons for her first," I say and go into the kitchen, hoping that the evening's conversation would be light, at least for Anna's sake.

"Marisha, why don't we write the letter tonight?" I hear Gabriella ask as I reach for the crayons in the kitchen drawer.

"Marisha, I'm worried for Anna." I hear Gabriella pleading as she's now standing in the kitchen doorway, waiting for my response.

"I promise you, Gabriella, I'll do everything possible to help," I say and hand Anna paper and some crayons.

When we sit down at the table, Anna scribbles pictures and tells us her stories about her school friends.

"Marisha, can I have some grape juice?" Anna gazes with her huge, brown eyes.

I always kept grape juice in my fridge for her. Today, the closest I have to grape juice is cranberry. When she takes a sip, her eyes squint. The memories of last Christmas come to my mind; Anna was so happy, filled with excitement, as she was unwrapping her gifts before her father's eyes. I try not to cry.

"Marisha, I'll write the letter, tomorrow," Gabriella says just before they leave.

***

Sleep is again illusive. Reluctantly, I take the painkillers and the anti-inflammatory. It takes time for them to do their job, but in the meantime I can't turn my head off. Sitting up in bed, I replay the events of the day and then finally drop into a troubled sleep, my journal on my breast. Not for long. The phone rings.

I pick up the receiver and note that the time is 11:30 P.M.

"Hello… hello… hello," I say louder and louder.

No answer. I panic as I hear only breathing on the other end of the line. I switch on the lamp and drop the phone when I see his number on the call display. Without delay, I dial the number given to me by Detective Strong.

A female voice comes on the line.

"May I please talk to Detective Strong?" I ask.

"Tonight, Detective Seaton is on duty."

"Then, can I please speak to Detective Seaton?"

"May I tell him who's calling?"

"Marisha Manley."

"Just a moment. I'll get him for you."

Detective Seaton immediately suggests that I dial *57 on my phone if Raffaele calls again.

"Make sure you do that," he says. "This way the police station will be alerted that he's making calls to you, and we'll definitely deal with him. For now, I'll get a cruiser to patrol your neighbourhood. I'm also making a note for Detective Strong to call you about this tomorrow."

"Thank you, Detective Seaton."

Am I ever going to get a restraining order against him? Can I sleep peacefully while in the grip of fear? Shall I expect another call from him, or will he appear on my doorstep?

My dear friend Ruth calls me this morning.

"How are you, Marisha?"

"I have tossed and turned all night. Instead of feeling rested, I'm totally exhausted by the nightmares," I say, thinking that counseling today might help me shake off my anxiety attacks.

Our conversation is a mere few words; my other line beeps.

"I'll talk to you later, Ruthie. There's another call from the *Toronto Star*."

"Good luck!" she says.

"Thanks!"

On the other line, a pleasant, friendly voice says,

"This is Donovan Vincent. Can I speak to Marisha Manley?"

"Pleased to meet you, Donovan. This is Marisha speaking."

Donovan cuts to the chase, "How do you feel about starting on your story?"

"I'm still weighing whether or not to tell my story to the press, but I need justice," I pause, thinking that when the story hits the newspapers, I'll be bombarded with questions from school administrators, students, and the public. Donovan Vincent says,

"If I don't get the story, someone else will."

He's right.

"When would you like to meet?"

"Is Wednesday at 10 A.M. convenient for you?"

"Okay," I reply, reluctantly.

While waiting for the call from Detective Strong, I settle on my living-room couch with the portable phone at arm's length, going over yesterday's events to prepare myself for the barrage of questions from the newspaper reporter. I am weighing to cancel the reporter's interview and keep my situation private or get fully prepared to live my life in a fishbowl. The ringing phone startles me.

"I hear he's been bothering you, again," Detective Strong says from the other end.

"He called twice last night around midnight."

"Make sure you use the *57. If he keeps calling you, he'll be stopped, immediately."

I'm gaining more and more trust in Detective Strong. His credibility and concern seem genuine.

"Detective Strong, what about my restraining order and what can be done about Gabriella's and Anna's safety?"

"It's a delicate situation. We'll have more answers after his probation officer interviews him. Please let Gabriella know that I'm pursuing this situation and I'll be in touch with her."

I'm hopeful that the crime will be presented before a judicial body, but I'm still troubled that he'll not be charged in Canada. I wonder if the media can help.

"Detective Strong, a reporter from the *Toronto Star* has asked me for an interview."

"The newspapers can report on the issue of the law but that will not help the investigation, at this stage. Make sure that the media's interest in your story is sincere."

Between the last two phone calls, I'm trying to get ready for my counseling session, which is at eleven, but the phone rings nonstop—next my mother, and then my daughter, Daniella, calling from England.

"Mom, I miss you so much. When are you're coming to visit me?" she asks.

I'm unable to give her an answer. It's too difficult to tell her the state of my affairs over the phone, how my life, in every possible way, has become so unpredictable. Right now Daniella is going through some difficulties with her fiancée, and I don't want to compound them. I simply tell her that I love her very much and I'll keep in touch with her regularly.

I'm late for counseling. It's almost eleven and I'm still driving up the hill on Yonge Street, instead of on the elevator to the fourth floor of the small office building. Julia is tired today; her daughter has been sick. She is still patiently attentive to me. I explain to her that Gabriella is asking me to help stop Raffaele from visiting their daughter, but that I can't do anything until the probation officer interviews Raffaele.

"You have enough of your own worries. Doesn't she understand that you can't help her until he's charged?"

"She kept asking me to write a letter to the probation officer, thinking that this will stop him from seeing Anna."

"Marisha, you need to take care of your own situation right now. This is stressing you out. Doesn't she understand?"

"I have promised Gabriella that I'll do everything I can to protect Anna."

Julia tells me, "Don't put any more stress on yourself than what you already have."

I thank her and mention that a reporter from the *Toronto Star* has asked me for an interview.

When I return home, Gabriella is waiting for me in the driveway.

"We must send a letter to his probation officer," she says frantically on the way to the porch.

153

"I feel the same urgency as you do, Gabriella, yet Detective Strong told me to wait until after he investigates," I object, as mildly as I can.

"But, Marisha, can't you see? I'm so worried about Anna," Gabriella argues.

I feel terrible to see her daughter included in our ongoing problem.

"Gabriella, I'm also very frustrated that we have to wait. But, let's consult Detective Strong and find out what our options are." I pick up the phone and dial him. He picks up the phone and after my brief report says: "Let me to talk to Gabriella."

I see Gabriella frowning during her conversation with him. We look at each other; our eyes reflect the same frustration.

"Yes, Detective Strong," I say after Gabriella hands me the phone.

"I need to ask you, if it's necessary, would you consider going back to Cuba to press charges against him, there?" Detective Strong asks.

"Yes, I would if I had to."

He informs me that my appointment with Hazel Walker is canceled for now.

"Detective Strong, Gabriella and I are still concerned for our safety," I say, as I come to the realization that our lives are in even more danger, now that he knows Gabriella and I are substantiating one another's cases.

"We'll have to wait till the end of this week," he says. "Remember, if he calls you again on your home phone, punch in *57. The police will be notified, immediately."

After our call, Gabriella again tells me her fears. She lets me know that she has warned Anna's daycare, just in case he tries to take Anna without her permission; each day she picks Anna up an hour earlier. We hug like estranged sisters, bonded only by the brutality of this perpetually violent man.

This evening, I write to my daughter, Daniella, in England. It's time that I tell her the truth about my ongoing situation. As a mother I have always tried to be open and honest with my daughters. Now, we are three adult women, each of us made strong by living 20 years of our lives together, through thick and thin.

However, I'm still their mother. I've nurtured, shielded, and protected them, preparing them as best as I knew how to allow them to fly. They have both embarked on their life's journey, secure that the focal point in their lives will always remain the same. For me now to lean on them emotionally is very hard. I seal the letter to Daniella, hoping that in these dark times I have the strength to provide her a ray of hope.

Chapter 13. Witnesses Statements

Detective Strong continues his duty with me, daily. This morning he arrives bright and early at 8:30.

"I have some good news," he says. "I met with his probation officer; he's scheduled for an interview tomorrow. I have more good news to tell you. Ottawa has been contacted, and an RCMP agent by the name of . . . , " he says, as my phone rings. I excuse myself and get up to answer the call.

"Hello," I say. "Yes, tomorrow will be much better for me." I hang up, thinking *I'm glad the reporter canceled the interview today* and I quickly return to the living room to hear the rest of Detective Strong's good news.

"Marcel Bouchette from the RCMP in Ottawa is going to be in touch with you," he says. "He's contacting Cuba to review the possibility of his extradition."

"Does this mean there's no possibility of him being prosecuted in Canada?" I ask as I can't bear the thought of someone else ending up in my current predicament.

"We don't know, Marisha. But we're trying everything possible."

I'm faced with the dilemma of confronting the irregularities of Canadian laws, knowing full well that perhaps the only way to achieve any justice, not just for myself but for future victims, would be to divulge my story to the press. I mention again to Detective Strong about the contact I had from the *Toronto Star.*

"Are you sure?" He's a bit hesitant about me going public, at this point.

"Detective Strong? I believe the media will only help."

"Please, have Donovan Vincent get in touch with me," Strong advises me and leaves quickly.

***

Next day at 10 A.M., a tall middle-aged man stands on my doorstep.

"I'm Donovan Vincent from the *Toronto Star.*"

"Pleased to meet you, Mr. Vincent."

"Please just call me 'Donovan.'"

The well-spoken reporter immediately tells me that the *Toronto Star's* law department has looked into my legal circumstances. His professional manner alleviates many of my fears about going public. He assures me that the press will only help.

The interview is lengthy and right to the point. Donovan asks many questions, beginning with the relationship.

"How would you describe your relationship with Raffaele?"

"As the relationship developed, he quoted passages about faith and how he loved me. On my birthday he gave me a diamond bracelet and 47 long-stemmed roses. The extra rose was for good luck, he told me." I stop for a moment and show the reporter the birthday card in which

Raffaele wrote these words, "My darling Marisha, you have enhanced my life."

The dynamic Donovan Vincent makes some more notes on his pad, quickly.

"Our families met," I continue. "He talked about getting married, buying a house."

I stop. Donovan Vincent waits for me to regain my composure.

"How did you and Raffaele end up going to Cuba?"

"The trip was a Christmas gift from him to me."

"Did you have any idea of his previous violence?"

"No. If I had known, I would never have spent any time with him, let alone been in a relationship with him. During the six months, he treated me well and that is why I accepted his invitation to travel with him to Cuba."

Donovan Vincent turns another recorded page, raises his head; his big brown eyes bring out sympathy, but time does not permit more worry about me. We have a more drastic situation to address; he continues, immediately,

"Please tell me about the holiday in Cuba."

I tell Donovan about the first night on the island, how the tone changed drastically.

"What day was this?"

"It was Monday, December 28." I answer. I notice he writes fast.

"Provide me with the details of what happened, that night."

I tell him that I had asked the Cubans to have him charged and to provide me with a return to Canada on the next available flight.

"Except, I stayed," I say, and pause because I feel nauseated as I think back on that event.

"Why did you stay?" the reporter asks.

"The resort management and the tour guide told me there was no flight until the following week." I almost start to cry, but then I force myself to go on telling the reporter how I got my own room and stayed there alone, until Raffaele came to spend the end-of-the-holiday night with me.

The reporter has recorded several pages of notes, and he doesn't seem to change gears; he keeps asking me about the details of that horrid last night of my holiday. While narrating my gruesome story, I feel like I will break down, but I press forward. His questions lead right to my current circumstances: the fact that now, in Canada, I'm unable to bring charges against my Canadian perpetrator.

The three hours of interview fly by. Donovan Vincent explains that it is his intention to contact both the Crown counsels and Detective Strong. When he departs, I feel exhausted, yet satisfied that I have made the right decision.

I add today's events to my journal; at the bottom of the page, I note:

I have never experienced anything like it before! I need to lie down; the pain in my neck is intense. My body craves rest but my mind won't permit it. It seems unnatural for me to become a victim, especially with my God-given tenacity!

Just as I lie down, the phone rings. It's Detective Strong.

"Marisha, I need to meet with you in person."

A half hour later, he arrives, and I usher him into the living room.

"By the way," he says, as he looks around the room. "Raffaele's probation officer told me that after she showed him the photos and after he was asked whether he'd committed the crime, he denied attacking you in Cuba."

I'm feeling nauseated and, at the same time, angry.

"Of course, he'll try everything not to go to jail; that's a given. I still have the problem of my personal protection. Where is my peace bond?"

"The law restricts the issuance of a restraining order until he's formally charged."

"But, Detective Strong, if we are unable to charge him, then what?"

"I have red dotted your area for now. Unfortunately, that's the only thing I can do. My hands are tied as well."

"I truly appreciate your efforts. Is there anything at this point that can restrict him from visiting Anna?"

"I've informed his probation officer about it. She's aware of Gabriella's concern for the child."

I'm taken aback, as I had hoped there would be a simple remedy and a temporary restraining order that could jointly allow both Gabriella and me to sleep at night.

"If there's a possibility of charging him, the Crown counsels in Newmarket will require witness statements, as soon as possible," Detective Strong says. "If they arrive by mail at your home, please call me immediately. I'll pick them up, personally."

Before leaving, he assures me that during the next week, the Crown counsels will be giving priority to my case. He goes on to explain that they are in uncharted territory. They are researching every possible case heard in the Canadian courts involving crimes committed abroad, by one Canadian against another. They hope to apply the relevant ones, arguing that if those cases were charged here in Canada, then the same can apply to mine.

That evening Gabriella phones.

"I would like to come over with Anna," she says.

I'm tired but I know we have a lot to discuss.

We recycle our common topic—his denial, his possible extradition, the Crown counsels' submitting my case, and the press involvement. While Gabriella and I talk, Anna colours her pictures at the living-room table. Gabriella and I return to the focal point, which is the urgency of protecting ourselves. We decide to jointly prepare a letter to his probation officer, mutually agreeing that we consult Detective Strong before we send it.

Next day Detective Strong visits me at my home. He again sits in the antique chair in my living room; it has become his chair now. Before he starts, I tell him of Gabriella's and my decision to write the letter to the probation officer. I feel relieved when he says that he agrees with it, but then asks that Gabriella send the letter by registered mail.

"It's better that it be official," he says and he opens his briefcase, smiles, removes a folder, and begins his narrative.

"We are fortunate that the Canadian people around you in Cuba have been so helpful." He sifts through a stack of papers. "The witness statements, especially Laurel's, are critical to your case."

I listen carefully as Detective Strong continues.

"The Crown counsel is preparing a brief to have your case heard."

"Brilliant!" I respond. I sense a breakthrough.

Then, Strong goes on to explain that the Crown counsel and her legal team are researching other cases to argue what should be charged in Canada. He points out that Laurel's affidavit is particularly helpful; her statement confirms that he admitted to the assault.

"Your case is starting to gain some legal ground."

"I hope so, Detective Strong."

"But I regret to inform you that there's still a problem getting the peace bond at this time. Technically, it can't happen until the Crown counsel takes the case to trial and only then can the judge issue it. In a meantime, be patient, Marisha."

I don't respond. Again, I'm disappointed.

He stares at his feet, knowing his hands are tied; nevertheless, he tries to offer a bit of consolation.

"You must understand, we're lucky in some ways. Your case has been given a great deal of attention. The Crown counsel is a damn adamant and believes you deserve justice."

His encouraging words are like a spoonful of sugar that helps the judicial medicine go down. However, there's still no remedy for my lack of protection.

"Detective, remember the press will be releasing my story soon."

"I'll keep you informed as to when the pre-trial is set. I'll call you, immediately. Meanwhile, rest and take care of yourself, and I'll talk to you soon."

***

After a month of visits at the hospital crisis unit, the social worker cannot nurse me back to mental health. Because she seems more frustrated, it worsens my feelings. The sessions with the psychologist promote my well-being: Julia listens to my grievances and focuses me to stay determined about my future.

Today, she's making sure that I prepare myself for the day in court, as I explain to her that it's rapidly approaching on March 4, 1999.

"I'm very thankful for Detective Strong's support and assistance. My knowledge of the judicial system is very limited; I've never even been inside a courtroom. Detective Strong has explained that this is only a pre-trial hearing, where Raffaele must appear before the judge as Detective Strong presents the evidence."

"No doubt, you must rest and not fret." She stops and then adds a few more caring words. "It seems as if the paperwork has begun, so you can relax a bit."

"Well, Detective Strong gave me copies of all the witness statements. I have to review them," I say, but I still think *how can I relax?*

In the evening, I laboriously review each witness affidavit, trying to stay strong and positive, as the psychologist has reminded me to do. The affidavits overwhelm me as they hold eight different perspectives, vividly described by each individual witness. But what exactly shall I do? What should be the plan of action?

Help comes from Detective Strong early in the morning. He sees me stumble into the living room.

"Gabriella has agreed to testify as one of the witnesses in court," he announces.

"That's wonderful!" I gain energy.

"The Crown counsel wants to meet with you to prepare you for the pre-trial."

"Great!"

"The Cubans have refused to have a foreign tourist tried in their country," he announces, and looking at me with regret, he continues, "External Affairs conclude that extradition and trial in Cuba are now completely out of the question."

I don't say anything.

The following day, Detective Strong is again on the scene. Before noon, he steers me through a maze of narrow hallways until we come to the side door of the Crown counsel's chambers. Next to her desk is an open file cabinet stuffed with bulky legal folders. The assistant Crown counsel, Marcy Henschell, is sitting at her desk, talking on the phone, coffee in hand. She doesn't look older than 22; confidence and positive energy flow out of her. She gives me a quick five-minute summary of the proposed research for my case.

"Marisha, how do you feel about this hearing?"

"I have never been in a courtroom before, and I'll have to see him, again. It will be tough on me."

"It's not really necessary for you to attend the preliminary hearing."

"I rather not, if you don't mind."

"There's a possibility that this case could be precedent-setting in the Canadian legal system."

"So, this preliminary hearing is for the purpose of ensuring a trial for my case?" I ask.

"Yes, That's right. The judge will decide whether or not his breach of the probation for his assault against his ex-wife can be tried." Henschell points to a pile of paperwork on her desk. "And, that'll mean we have a trial. I hope the judge at the preliminary hearing will also issue you a 12-month restraining order."

"Will his breach of probation be enough to put him away?"

"This is why we're going into the pre-trial hearing," the Crown counsel says.

"Thank you, Ms. Henschell."

"You're welcome."

We shake hands and Detective Strong and I leave her office and enter the long hallway. We don't waste any time and walk, quickly, through a deluge of chaotic sounds, loud conversations, bangs, even some cries. It seems that only the lawyers are happy to be here. I can't take crowds anymore; I seem to be developing claustrophobia.

Finally outside, I rush through a full parking lot. My car is parked at the far end. I can't wait to be inside it.

Chapter 14. Preliminary Hearing

Finally, it's March 4, 1999.

Grecci's preliminary hearing is in progress in closed chambers at the Ontario Court of Justice in Newmarket. Today, Mr. Justice Vibert A. Lampkin decides if sufficient evidence exists for my case to be tried in Canadian courts. The hearing's issue is whether "Raffaele Grecci can be charged in Canada on the basis that he has failed, without a reasonable excuse, to comply with the terms of his probation order."

I look at my watch. 11 A.M. Two minutes later than my last time check. I stand up and start pacing around my living room, throwing glances at the phone on the end table. It rests in silence. I sit down; every movement makes my legs hurt, and my nerves are irritated to the max. Why hasn't Detective Strong called? Maybe Ralph didn't show up. What will I do if my case does not go to court and he goes free, unpunished? Maybe the judge tossed the case out, and Strong is hesitating to call me. No, that doesn't make any sense. Detective Strong has always been upfront. Maybe . . . wait a minute! I try to corral my thoughts. Breathe, Marisha, I tell myself. It's like gulping in the last air on earth.

Then, I remember that Donovan Vincent, the attentive to my case and a diligent reporter for the *Toronto Star,* said to me he would be at the hearing to get the story. That's good, or is it? How am I going to handle the whole world, at least the Toronto area, knowing what happened to me? How will . . . Breathe, Marisha, I tell myself. But I need to peek at my watch. Nearly noon. What is going on?

The phone finally rings. I jump to answer it. The cord tangles, sending the base sprawling onto the floor. I don't care; the voice at the other end is much more important. Detective Strong announces,

"Justice Lampkin says that your case is more complex than it first appeared to be." He pauses and I can hear the loud bustle of a courtroom around him. I wait for him to tell me more. "Marisha, his lawyer is arguing that the court lacks jurisdiction to try him for his offence in Canada."

"But, I need protection from him. I live in constant fear, Detective Strong." I grip the phone.

"Justice Lampkin does not want Grecci to get away with the crime, so he has granted a pre-motion on April 8."

The legal dilemma has now escalated, and I feel as if I'm still standing at the beginning of a long battle. I need to arm myself to fight. God, give me the strength!

Then, Detective Strong tries to encourage me.

"I'll be dropping off the application forms for you to file at the office of the Canadian Criminal Injuries Compensation Board." He adds, "It's to help you financially."

"Thank you. I appreciate your help," I say, realizing this compensation is one support in my fight.

"Don't mention it," he answers.

Detective Strong tries very hard to help me survive this awful time in my life. Today, he hands me a brown envelope containing the application to the Canadian Criminal Injuries Compensation Board.

"I hope that the compensation will relieve you financially from all of the extra expenses, which you're incurring now," he says.

Indeed, unexpected expenses have blindsided me this month. I have incurred lawyer fees, medical expenditures, and other unusual costs. Neither my work benefits nor the borrowed funds against my mortgage loan have arrived. I'm preoccupied with how I'll survive financially.

"The Crown counsels are preparing more documentation for the pre-motion," he states. Then, I let him know that the reporter from the *Toronto Star* will be doing an in-depth interview with me.

"Yes, Donovan was talking to me, yesterday," he says.

I thank Detective Strong for the visit and his diligent work.

"Don't even mention it," he responds, as he leaves.

***

Fear, like a thick wall locking me in, surrounds me wherever I go, whatever I do, and with whomever I speak. Even in my home, I can't find tranquility. I fear. The phone ringing jerks me up. I hope that whoever is calling can lift me out of this horrible mess or at least away from these dismal feelings.

It's Donovan Vincent, and as I listen to him speak, I start to get excited.

"I have been sitting through the preliminary hearing today," he tells me.

"Would you mind if we meet, again? I want to get more information from you and complete an in-depth interview for the article in our newspaper."

From reading some of his other stories, Donovan Vincent seems to have a reputation for a crusader style of journalism, attentive to the rights of the public.

"For sure," I reply to him. "I can't wait for the story in the newspaper."

I remind myself that patience is a virtue; I'm trying to keep my head above water in a pool filled with fear and injustice.

Later in the afternoon, my hand aches from hours of filling out the twelve-page government application. The actual scribbling presents the least of my pain; it's the content that draws emotional blood. The forms require that I document my injuries. Some of it has already been recorded elsewhere, thank God; now, I only need to type it out, but my mind still relives the gruesome attack, and I must collect and attach all of my doctors' and specialists' medical statements.

Ruth is on the phone with me for a short time, and then she drops by after work for a moment. I always welcome her smile and energetic nature. She brought a printout of a case reported in the newspaper about a victim (Canadian male) who was gravely assaulted by his business partner (Canadian male) in Haiti.

"Isn't this a coincidence?" she asks. "The victim is also unable to charge the crime in Canada." She picks up the top form of the twelve-page application to the Canadian Criminal Injuries Compensation Board and tries to encourage me. "Marisha! The compensation should help you, at least financially."

"Yes, I hope so, Ruth. I need it very badly."

In a matter of a week, I open the long white envelope from the Canadian Criminal Injuries Compensation Board with impatient hands, sure to read something good, at last.

The letter informs me how naïve we are. Here is what I read:

Dear Ms. Manley,

Your request to the Board for a CICB claim package has been considered.

To be eligible for compensation from the Criminal Injuries Compensation Board, you must have been the victim of a crime of violence that occurred in Ontario and you must have sustained injury as a result of that crime. Enclosed, for your information, is a copy of Section 5 of the Compensation for Victims of Crime Act.

What? I shake the letter as if I'm holding the tail of a snake. I'm furious. I have hit another brick wall; bureaucratic red tape has now compounded the pain of the vicious physical beating. I continue reading.

Unfortunately, as the incident occurred outside of Ontario, you are ineligible to apply for compensation with our Board. Thus, we are unable to process your request for an application.

Yours truly,

Sylvio Asti, Compensation Administrator
I guess I was wrong in my optimism. The bureaucracy of the Canadian judicial system begins to loom in my mind as a merciless adversary. Anger pushes me to dial the manager of the Compensation Board.

"He's quite busy, and unavailable at this time," the nonchalant woman on the other end of the line says.

"Please! Let me speak to Mr. Asti. I have a very important case for him."

"I'll see if I can put you through to his secretary."

I patiently wait, hoping perhaps if I talk about my situation, person-to-person, I can change the decision.

"Hello, this is Diane, Mr. Asti's secretary. What can I do for you?"

"My name is Marisha Manley. I would like to ask Mr. Asti if he could look into my application more carefully."

She listens to my case and takes my name and phone number.

"I'll have him call you, as soon as possible."

"When? Today?" I ask.

Mr. Asti actually returns my call soon. After I tell him my circumstances, I ask if my application could be reviewed.

"No. It's impossible," he replies. "The CCICB operates only under provincial jurisdiction."

But I plead my case.

"The person who committed this crime against me is from Ontario, and so am I."

"What is written on the paper before me is that compensation for victims of crime according to Section 5 of the Act is provided only to those whose crime occurs in the province of Ontario."

"We're both Ontarians. And I cannot be compensated here in Ontario?"

Another long pause occurs.

"I agree with you," he says with official sympathy. "I think the Act should read, 'A person from any province in Canada who has been a victim of a violent crime, outside the province or the country, is compensated if they have been injured as a result of that crime.' But it does not. This is the law as it stands. Under Section 5 of the Act, victims are compensated only 'within each province.'"

"Do you mean that if this crime had happened in Alberta, I could not be compensated in Ontario?"

"Yes. This is right."

"What do you suggest I do in my case?" I ask Mr. Asti.

"Perhaps, the best thing is to contact the Cuban Embassy and see if they will compensate you."

"Mr. Asti . . . " I hesitate for a few moments and then slam down the receiver for the lack of words.

If Mr. Asti is serious, as he is supposed to be as a government official, I wonder what education and IQ are required for government jobs? Cuba is a communist country and one of the poorest in the world. My injuries have been committed by another Canadian. How come this has nothing to do with the crime? If he is the right person for the Compensation Board, then he would save lots of money for the government.

Chapter 15. Nationwide Media Attention

My living room is being used by Donovan Vincent from the *Toronto Star* to wrap up the interviews. He has already followed my case through the preliminary hearing. No matter how committed I am to having the interview completed, it's draining to retell the events in Cuba. At the end of the interview, I've reached the point of physical nausea. Still a photographer shows up at my house to take pictures. In passing conversation, he relays to me some of the difficulties he's had catching Raffaele on film.

"He was trying to run away from me; finally, I got him with a telephoto lens at the back of his office," he says, and I'm thinking the obvious; he will not get away with this crime!

"May I use these two photos?" Donovan Vincent points to one of Raffaele and me as a "happy-looking couple" two days before the end of the Cuban holiday, and the other of me after his attack.

"Sure," I reply, although I know what to expect tomorrow.

"Your story is going to print tonight," Donovan says.

Then he gathers his papers as the photographer clicks a few shots of me in my living room. They both scurry out the front door, hoping to beat the rush-hour traffic back to their office.

***

The next day starts with a rainy morning. Before I get my morning paper, there's already a call.

"Marisha, check it; it's front-page news," Ruth says.

I run to my front doorstep; I feel a surge of adrenaline rush through my body. A clear-blue plastic bag contains the Saturday newspaper. I shake off the beads of water and head back to my living-room table.

I raise my eyes from the front page as I unfurl the *Toronto Star* and look at rain streaking down the window; its reflection on the living-room walls seems to mirror my despair.

The *Toronto Star* headline reads in bold print:

One Woman's Quest for Justice—Teacher Wins Day in Court After Case Is Snarled in Red Tape.

I cringe as the truth is recorded in print above photos on the front page of the most popular newspaper in my beloved city. I still shake when I see them. I don't know if it's the loss of privacy or if I'm reliving the ordeal.

One picture, of Raffaele and me, depicts us as two happy, smiling vacationers. An overlapping police photo of my brutally beaten face is inserted. The photos are like a macabre "before and after" for a weight-loss program. The caption underneath the photos reads, *Romantic holiday ends in savage beating. Six days into the holiday, there is an attack; her face was left a bloodied pulp.*

I touch my face, feeling the roughness of the scar tissue, now partially healed. I read on. *The nightmare of this holiday today—it's now 76 days later and it's nowhere near over.*

I have always taken pride in being an educator, instructing others not to be violent or victimized, in any way. What a joke!

I continue reading the article—another full-page spread on A17, explaining the details of my story—basically, everything the reporter recorded during the interviews with me. *The assault followed accusation by her attacker that she had shown interest in other men.*

The reporter wrote the truth, but the article doesn't say that Raffaele Grecci's accusation is a lie. I would never have looked at another man, or even thought about another man, when I was so in love with Raffaele. When I read his lie now in bold print, I'm filled with so much pain.

Yet, I know that I have agreed to have my story printed for good reasons—to protect myself with the truth about the crime, to expose my complex legal situation, and hopefully to receive justice. I know that Raffaele will lie, incessantly, as the case will be documented in newspapers for thousands upon thousands to read.

I compose myself, straighten the paper, and read on. Raffaele led the journalist on a merry chase out the back door of his office, and when the journalist finally caught up with him, lied.

"Absolutely nothing. Absolutely nothing," Grecci told Donovan. *"We had separate rooms. We had separate rooms."*

My hands shake; my eyes water as I place the article on the coffee table. I stare at my phone; I know that at any moment it will start ringing and continue ringing nonstop. I dread the thought of having to respond to my new horrible notoriety—not only his blatant lies but also, more

importantly, why my ordeal to charge him is only
beginning.

My sole consolation is to focus on my reason for
revealing my story; I hope that when the public read the
article, they'll become aware of the truth, which is why I'm
putting myself under this painful public microscope.
Donovan writes:

*The case is complicated, involving jurisdictional
issues, and it is also clouded by legal advice. Cuban
officials advised Manley that she should charge her
attacker in Canada.*

The article speaks the cold truth.

Under the Criminal Code, *a Canadian victim cannot
charge another Canadian for a crime that took place
outside the country! Only limited exceptions are provided*!

In the scope of Canadian jurisdiction, now I know
why, although a Canadian citizen, I do not fit under that
"limited exception" under the *Criminal Code of Canada*, as
the article explains. I have researched this legality. I am not
protected internationally because I have not been a victim
of an aircraft hijacking; I have not been taken hostage; I
have not been tortured or injured by nuclear materials; I
have not been victimized by a war crime, or piracy, and I
am not a Canadian civil servant.

What most alarms me about the article is this
statement that the reporter managed to get out of Raffaele.

*"There won't even be a trial because there was no
breach of probation. I always kept the peace. I'm a very
peaceful man. I carry a picture of my daughter."*

I wonder if I will ever be freed from the current
shackles of injustice and legal complexities that now rule

my life. I foresee travel on a very rocky road for a long, long time.

I'm thankful that the reporter has done his homework. In the article, he further explains: *The Crown counsel, Gillian Roberts, plans to argue in a pre-trial motion that although the offender can't be charged in Canada for the assault in Cuba, Grecci did breach his Canadian-issued probation order, dated May 7, 1997, for assaulting his ex-wife. Conditions of the order included requirements that he not assault anyone else and that he keep the peace for two years.*

Donovan Vincent also quotes Detective Eric Strong, York Regional Police.

"Manley didn't get this far in her battle without frustration and anguish. Numerous police officers and justices of the peace in Greater Toronto refused to touch her case for weeks. This case needs to be investigated and prosecuted to the fullest extent of Canadian law."

I am deeply thankful that Detective Strong and the Crown counsel, Gillian Roberts, have taken it upon themselves to champion my cause.

The first phone call comes from Ruth. There's anger in her voice as she reads from the paper.

"Cuban authorities didn't charge him, allowed him to leave, and haven't requested that he return. The department of foreign affairs has been in contact with the victim. Can you believe that, Marisha! Listen to this! *We are reviewing the case with Canadian police officials."*

"Ruth, imagine if he wasn't on probation. His breach of it is the only legal recourse I have to charge him."

"Yeah! And on top of it all, they have to wait for a decision on the jurisdiction to back this motion. This is nuts."

"Ruth, if I had been a victim of an aircraft hijacking, taken hostage, tortured, injured by nuclear materials, victimized by a war crime, or piracy, or a Canadian civil servant, then I would have been given justice!"

"But you have been brutally victimized and both of you are Canadians!"

"Yes, that's true!"

I file the article in a folder; I don't realize that many more will follow.

Chapter 16. Public Indignation

It's the first day back at my high school, after the holiday from hell. I wonder if I will be able to cope with the rigours of daily teaching. I feel nervous because my story has become public knowledge.

I climb the three flights of stairs, quickly unlock the door, and ask a small crowd of students to wait in the hallway. Inside the classroom, I place my briefcase and the stack of papers on the desk as neatly as possible, while the students are eagerly trying to enter. For sure many of them have already read the news. After the second bell, I pull myself together and let them in.

"Could you all take your assigned seats?" I say, as the students bounce into the room.

As I start my lesson, the class is unusually silent. Many questioning eyes stare at me, as if seeing my face for the first time. At some point I am so exhausted that I have to sit down to rest my spirit and my injured leg.

"If you need me, please let me know," I say.

Kefa, a student from Ghana, raises her hand. I have always had fun listening to her interesting stories. She was born into a wild tribe, people literally living in a stone age. From childhood she has had a passion for knowledge. It is fascinating to hear how she escaped from the tribe, found her way to Europe, and then to Canada.

"Yes, Kefa," I say.

"I'm terribly sorry for being so tactless, Miss
Manley," she says, struggling with shyness, "but I can't
help asking you a question. I'm sure everyone here wants
to know. Is it really true that there's no Canadian law to
charge a Canadian who assaults another outside Canada?"
        "I'm afraid so. It's not that simple."
        "Simple or not, how about protection? Even that does
not exist for you?" she insists.
        "True. I can't believe it myself," I say.
        "How idealistic I was," Kefa continues. "When I came
to Canada, I believed in the law and order in this country.
Somehow, it is even worse than in my jungle. Although no
law exists there, at least my tribesmen would beat the hell
out of him, legal system or not. I see that the law protects
him better than you; if someone would like to avenge you,
this person would be severely punished?"
        Suddenly, everyone speaks at once. I am surprised
how devoted to justice and truth they are! A tall, blond
student tries to break through the noise at the top of his
lungs.
        "You taught us, Miss Manley, that Canada is a
democratic country, which enjoys a worldwide reputation
for upholding human rights. Which human rights? Now it
upholds the rights of your attacker. He is the one who's
protected, not you. It blows my mind!"   I raise my hand
and the class returns to silence. However, I don't have a
chance to say a word.
        "Miss Manley, how come there's no law for this
violent crime?" a female voice from the last row asks. "If
we students feel that this hideous crime should be punished,
how come the Canadian justice system doesn't?"

"Hold on, hold on," I say. "I can't explain to you the law that, as you say, protects the criminal. But I believe in my country. I assure you that I will continue my fight for justice."

What can I say to them? From their textbooks, my students have learned that the purpose of the criminal law, as it applies to one's safety, ideally is designed to ensure the safety of all, while upholding the standards of decency and public order. I have taught and endlessly expounded upon these virtues and privileges granted to us by the democratic country we live in. Now the shape of my face, and newspaper articles, tell the opposite.

I look up at the clock as the final bell rings. Again, it startles me. I quickly gather papers, pick up my coat, and rush out. When in the car, I weave my way out of the school parking lot straight for counseling.

"My case has become the talk of the town," I tell her, eager to hear her comments. "My newfound notoriety brings me in direct contact with people who normally would be only casual acquaintances. They all emphasize how stunned they are after seeing the graphic photos of my beating displayed on the front page of the *Toronto Star*."

"Your story has extensive press coverage. We have a few copies of the paper here in our waiting room."

"It snowballed. Phone calls and e-mails are pouring in to the newspaper. My private number is now public, and the phone rings nonstop."

"How is this affecting you?"

"Well, I have had callers tell me that they are shocked after reading the newspaper articles. Many Canadians travel on holiday to exotic places like Cuba. How unfortunate for

Canadians if these countries become tropical paradises for
Canadian criminals."

"True!"

"There's nothing we can do?" I say and look for some
answers.

"It's incredible that our judicial system has such a
crack!"

"Another caller with a note of laughter in his voice
said, 'I have a brilliant idea. Please tell it to the reporters. I
think that this loophole in the Canadian law is a good
vehicle for Canadians to initiate an uncontested divorce.
Ah?'"

"Would you believe this?" the psychologist sighs and
shakes her head, I add one more comment,

"One of the people who called said that even if
Canada cannot establish a treaty with Cuba, Canadians
should initiate a law to protect its citizens who travel to
exotic countries!"

I get home in a much better mood. As soon as I open
the door, the phone rings. This time, it is Donovan Vincent,
the reporter from the *Toronto Star*, who now has become
my most trusted contact in the media. We now call one
another by our first names.

"Lots of people want to help you financially by setting
up a trust fund," he says. This heart-warming gesture
moves me.

"I'm pleased to hear it," I say, "but I need to keep any
media focused on my cause, to obtain justice. I have to at
least try to increase public awareness, and then maybe an
amendment to the *Criminal Code of Canada* may occur so

that in the future others will not be affected by this common legal dilemma."

One call delighted me immensely.

"The only way to gain justice is to actively petition for an amendment to the *Criminal Code of Canada,*" a woman on the other end of the line says.

"Coincidences? Chances? Miracles! They never stop!"

"Especially, if you start the ball rolling," she adds.

"Of course. How do I start?"

"There are a lot of people who want to touch base with you. Can I offer my secretary to work out a schedule with you?"

Now, I'm overwhelmed.

"I'm available anytime after three," I say.

How do you organize a petition to amend a law? I scribble a few thoughts in my notebook and then, impatient and exited, I grab a leftover sandwich from the fridge, take my first bite, dial my detective friend, and cut straight to the chase.

"I'm glad you're in, Detective Strong. I'm trying to draft a legal petition to the House of Commons."

"Aren't you having any lunch today?" He laughs a bit. His words cheer me up.

"People are responding to the newspaper article. They are suggesting I initiate a petition."

"This is good. Make sure you don't overwork yourself."

I read the first draft of the proposed petition to him.

"The petition aims at enabling a victim of a crime to be able to lay criminal charges when a serious criminal

offence takes place outside Canada and when both of the
parties are Canadian."
"Marisha, good for you," he says.
My energy seems to rise as he continues.
"Your MP is your best bet."
"Detective Strong, I'd better run now."
"If you need more help, call me," he says.
"Thank you, again!"
"Don't mention it," he replies, as always.
I hang up the phone and, with a surge of energy, get
back to writing the petition.
I'm happy for the media's unprecedented support and
very thankful for the positive response of my community; it
makes me believe I'm doing something special. I dial the
number to The Honourable Elinor Caplan, my local
Member of Parliament. At first, I have difficulty
introducing myself on the phone, but once the secretary
connects my name to the face in the newspaper article, she
immediately transfers my call to Jennifer Stone, the
assistant to my MP. She, like many others, knows the legal
complexity of my case. Soon she lets me know that my
meeting with Elinor Caplan will take place in two days.
On the scheduled day, my local MP welcomes me into
her office.
"It's a good idea, Marisha. I promise that my office
will submit the petition, once it exceeds the 2,500 required
signatures. You must take the proper legal steps though.
First, write a personal letter to the Minister of Justice
regarding your case and the reason for the proposed
petition. I would include the newspaper article with it.

Then, the office of the Attorney will respond with the legal forms for you to start the petition."

Now, however, despite such powerful support, I'm a bit reluctant to become too positive; I don't want my hopes raised and dashed again.

Next day, I hand Jennifer Stone a large envelope containing a brief letter along with a copy of the documentation of my injuries. She explains to me that the response from Ottawa will take a week or two.

"There's a short time frame, Marisha. You legally have only one week to gather petitions," she says.

Chapter 17. Legally, not Protected!

The big day, April 8, 1999, arrives!

It's three in afternoon; I'm in the staff room, photocopying handouts for the next lesson plans. The school secretary pages me on the intercom.

"Marisha, there's a call for you."

I run behind the divider to receive the anticipated call in privacy.

"I'm still at the courthouse," Strong announces.

"Today, the Crown counsel Gillian Roberts and Crown counsel assistant Marcy Henschell argued that Grecci could be charged with breach of his probation. On May 21, Justice Lampkin will make the decision whether your case goes to trial," he adds with optimism.

"Wow! Finally, there's a break! Does this mean that I'll get my restraining order?"

"It looks good. I'll deliver Robert's pre-trial motion papers later today, if you'll be at home." Strong relays.

Later in the evening, I focus with great frustration on the eight-page legal document before me. The legal language becomes more obscure and confusing; I feel lost in its intricacy.

Ruth somehow knows when to show up, even though she arrives unannounced.

"Good timing," I welcome her. "Maybe you can help me understand this twisted legal lingo."

And I read aloud:

"MEMORANDUM

SUMMARY OF THE SUBMISSIONS OF THE CROWN

Breach of probation is founded at section 733.1 of the *Criminal Code*. It provides that:

733.1 (1) An offender who is bound by a probation order and who, without reasonable excuse, fails or refuses to comply with that order is guilty of

(a) an indictable offence and is liable to imprisonment for a term not exceeding two years; or

(b) an offence punishable on summary conviction and is liable to imprisonment for a term not exceeding eighteen months, or to fine not exceeding two thousand dollars, or both.

(2) An accused who is charged with an offence under subsection (1) may be tried and punished by a court having jurisdiction to try that offence in the place where the offence is alleged to have been committed or in the place where the accused is found, is arrested, or is in custody, . . . "

I look to Ruth for some explanation.

"Can you make any sense of this?"

"Yes, I can."

I'm relieved; she replies further,

"In a nutshell, it means that Ralph breached his probation order, and for this particular offence, it seems that it doesn't matter where the breach occurred. He was bound by a probation order, period. You might have a good chance, Marisha."

"Good chance?" I cry. "Nothing is for sure!"

"I'm afraid not." Ruth shrugs her shoulders and, noticing my frustration, tries to soothe me.

"Look, Marisha, we are mere vestiges of our colonial past. It's not easy to shake off its stupidity. Please let me read on," Ruth suggests, and she does.

"The *Ouellette* case *(Tab 5)* is of particular assistance in an analysis of the case because it is factually similar to the matter. In *Ouellette, supra*, the accused and the victim went to the Dominican Republic on a holiday. A dispute occurred during which the accused struck the victim and caused her to fall to the ground. The victim lost consciousness in the Dominican. She was transported back to Quebec, and died in Canada five days after having been struck. Some of the witnesses were in the Dominican Republic and some were in Quebec. The families of both the victim and the accused were in Quebec. The accused was charged with assault to commit bodily harm in the Dominican Republic. The charges were still pending at the time of the consideration of the jurisdiction issue in Canada. The Dominican Government indicated that they would seek his extradition if not tried in Canada. However, the Dominican Republic would be satisfied if the accused was tried in Canada."

"Wow! Ruthie, this case is so close to mine."

"Marisha, listen to this. 'The court in the *Ouellette* case concluded that without the death of the victim the offence of manslaughter could not be laid, so the death was a determinant element of the offence.'"

"The girl died. Nicely put: 'Death was the determinant element of the offence.' This means that if he had killed me, then he would have been charged!"

"I can't imagine to have had this happen to me."

"Exactly! Under the current law, only murdered people deserve justice. If you are not dead, forget it. His probation order is your only chance."

"But under the best circumstances, he would be charged with no more than a year in prison!" I cry.

"Try your best!" Ruth says. "Hopefully, publicity and public outcry will make our government consider the will of people, whom supposedly it serves."

Ruth leaves; I revisit the documents. I thank the Crown counsel, Gillian Roberts and Crown counsel assistant Marcy Henschell, for researching so diligently the archives of the *Criminal Code of Canada.* I can only hope now that Mr. Justice Lampkin will grant a trial, at least for Grecci's breach of probation.

Chapter 18. Extended Media Frenzy

The media frenzy that followed was like a huge fireworks display, which almost blinded everyone who was involved in, or was familiar with, my case. I wasn't able to put it in proper sequence, as it changed like a huge kaleidoscope, sensitive to the slightest touch of a finger. It began with a headline in the morning edition of the *Toronto Star*.

Man Breaches Probation in Cuba, Crown Argues—1997 Order Extends Beyond Canada's Borders, Judge Told in Unusual Case.

The case is unusual because under the Criminal Code of Canada *an individual cannot be charged with a crime that happened outside Canada, with limited exceptions.*

Grecci's probation extends beyond Canada's borders.

The reporter quotes Crown counsel, Gillian Roberts's argument, *Where else could he be held accountable for breaching a probation order but in Canada?*

In argument to determine whether the case goes to trial, Crown counsel Gillian Roberts argued that Grecci can be charged with violating conditions of his probation order issued May 7, 1997, when Grecci was convicted of assaulting his ex-wife. The probation order required he keep the peace and maintain good behaviour.

Cuba has not asked Grecci to return to face charges, the court was told. As there is no extradition treaty between Canada and Cuba, Grecci would need to, voluntarily, return to Cuba if officials there chose to prosecute him.

Henschell cited Supreme Court and lower court decisions where crimes involving Canadians were committed outside the country, yet the courts felt Canada had the jurisdiction to prosecute.

A barrage of questions from my students, co-workers, and friends does not leave me the time for rest. The petitions are piling up. In a few days, over 1,500 people have signed them. *Toronto Star* readers daily petition people on the street. Something is going to happen, I am sure.

The press does not stop embracing my "complicated" case. A CITY-TV reporter contacts me, asking for an interview with the network; I agree to have my case broadcast on the evening news.

At 6 P.M., the report hits the airwaves. The announcer issues a public warning:

What you're about to see now are very graphic pictures of a victim who was brutally beaten by her boyfriend in Cuba. She returned to Canada to learn that she is unable to charge him with the crime committed against her.

A snapshot, taken by Steve Joyce in Cuba, of my swollen face, covered with blood and cuts, appears on the screen. The commentator continues:

A law here does not cover this horrid assault in Canada. It has to do with jurisdiction. The victim is using every possible means to seek justice for the crime committed against her.

The petition exceeds 2,500 signatures already. Incredible!

The following day, while I am submitting the petitions to my MP, The Honourable Elinor Caplan, once again CITY-TV broadcasts my story. This report brings my case up to date. This time, it tells about not only my struggle to obtain justice, but also about a petition to the Minister of Justice to amend a law so that other Canadians don't have to go through the same injustice.

At the end of the afternoon, when I reach my driveway, JoJo Chin, a crime reporter from CITY-TV, is already interviewing Monica. He must have arrived as she was stuffing my mailbox with more petitions.

The camera turns toward me.

"Miss Manley, you're submitting these petitions to your MP's office today. Is that right?" the reporter asks.

"That's right."

"What are you hoping to accomplish?"

"I'm trying to have a law in the *Criminal Code of Canada* amended. The law would enable Canadian victims of a crime to lay charges against another Canadian when a serious criminal offence takes place outside Canada."

At 6 P.M., the network televises the report from the office of my local MP. This time the announcer states:

We are following up on the story of a Canadian woman who has been brutally beaten by her Canadian boyfriend, in Cuba. A law here does not cover the assault that occurred in Cuba in Canada and the victim is seeking justice.

The reporter comes up to me, holding his mike close to my lips.

These petitions are part of your search for justice?

"Yes," I say into the mike. "*Justice for myself and hopefully to spare others the ordeal that I am now going through! These petitions are a demand to amend the law.*"

The news segment wraps up with my local MP, The Honourable Elinor Caplan, accepting the petitions and promising me to have them tabled in the House of Commons, before the Minister of Justice.

My problematic case is on the right track, but still, everything will be riding on Judge Lampkin's ruling. The media feel the same way and closely follow every move of each player of this real-time drama. The *Toronto Star* prints:

Judge Decides Probation Order Extends Beyond Canada's Border.

Wow!

***

The following day, May 21, 1999, I open the *Toronto Star*, turn to page two, and read the report on the court ruling. In bold print I read:

Accused in Cuba, He Faces a Trial Here.

And, again, the story carries the same police photo of my attacker.

The first sentence of the article, which reads, *Grecci has denied he assaulted Manley when the two were vacationing at a Cuban resort Jan. 4,* does not affect me any more. I read on:

Justice Vibert A. Lampkin of the Ontario Court of Justice, in an extraordinary move rules, "Grecci's probation order required that he behave, while he was abroad, as well as in Canada. When there is a probation order against a citizen requiring him to keep the peace and be of good behaviour, then it is therefore, doubly important that he observe the terms of the order when he is in a foreign country."

The Crown counsel, Gillian Roberts, has argued successfully *"that the probation order follows the probationer wherever he goes."*

There is a real and substantial link between the offence and Canada, because the probation order was made in Canada.

The articles goes on to explain that his criminal lawyer, Mr. Sonito, has argued that, *"The probation order—issued after Grecci was convicted May 7, 1997, in Brampton for assaulting his ex-wife—did not require that his client keep the peace in another country."*

However, Judge Lampkin has dismissed this argument and granted a trial, scheduled in September.

***

The following day brings more good news. The Crown counsel, armed with Judge Lampkin's ruling, prepares a letter of appeal to the Canadian Criminal Injuries Compensation Board:

Policy Analyst
Criminal Injuries Compensation Board
4th Floor
439 University Avenue
Toronto, ON M5G 1Y8

Dear Sirs/Madam,
Re: Marisha Manley Claim
I am the Crown counsel, who has the carriage of the matter of **R. v. Raffaele Grecci.** *Ms. Manley is the complainant in the matter. The incident relates to an extreme assault, which occurred in Cuba. Mr. Raffaele Grecci was bound by a probation order at the time of the occurrence. His Honour Judge Vilbert A. Lampkin has ruled that the Ontario court has jurisdiction to try Mr. Grecci for the offence of breach of probation. Consequently, Ms. Marisha Manley is a victim/witness in relation to that charge.*

I have enclosed a copy of the ruling of Judge Lampkin in relation to the issue of jurisdiction. The next scheduled court appearance for Mr. Grecci is November 22, 1999. If you have any questions please contact me.
Marcy Henschell
Assistant Crown counsel

***

The sun is shining brighter than ever on this first day of June. I run in from my backyard to catch the phone call.

With excitement, I pick up the receiver. Jennifer Stone, the assistant at MP Caplan's office, announces,

"Marisha, I've got some good news. Karen Kirk, the MP for York North constituency, has tabled your petition before the House of Commons."

"That's excellent," I reply, and a surge of hope enters my heart that the law will be amended. This would not be for me but at least for others.

"Now, we'll just wait for the Minister of Justice to make her decision," Jennifer says.

At that time I hoped that the wishes of ordinary people would be a part of the Minister of Justice's considerations. I trusted . . . but a new, nerve-wracking experience was in the cards: THE TRIAL!

Chapter 19. Rough Days in Court

I crave a fresh start. The ever-pressing daily reminders of my case, even in my workplace, don't allow me any break. Eight months ago when I made the decision to pursue justice, I thought I knew what to expect. Today, however, I'm wondering if I bit off more than I can chew. It's September 28, a red-letter day. I'm trembling with the thought of confronting my attacker in person for the first time since I watched him walk away scot-free from the authorities at Pearson International Airport.

Early this morning Detective Strong meets Katrina, Dan, and me at the doors of the Newmarket Courthouse. The detective continues to do his best to protect me; today, he keeps my exposure to Grecci to the minimum. He makes sure I don't confront Grecci in the hallway by quickly escorting Katrina, Dan, and me through the etched-glass doors bearing the words, *Victims and Witnesses Waiting Room.* Then, he leaves us, until I'm summoned into the courtroom.

The walls of the small victims and witnesses waiting room are closing in on me. I open my folder to review the notes that I've written for today. I'm unable to focus; my eyes shift, sporadically checking the time on the large clock above the door. I feel another nervous yawn coming on. My

throat is dry no matter how many tiny paper cups of water
Alice hands me. I spring to my feet to assure myself I still
have circulation in my legs. I'm filled with apprehension as
the court time draws near. I hope that presiding Justice
Vibert A. Lampkin will discover some issue on the
application that will enable him to prosecute Grecci, if not
for the crime committed against me, at least for his breach
of the probation order.

Finally, Detective Strong announces, "It's time."

Alice puts her arm around me. "I know it's hard," she
says as I'm having difficulty walking, "but you must be in
the courtroom, right now."

I follow Detective Strong. With Katrina and Dan, we
all march over the threshold, my eyes turn neither left nor
right. Ominous silence greets us. The only sound resonating
in my ears is the metallic click of the soundproof door,
firmly shutting behind us. I sit between Katrina and Alice,
flanked by Detective Strong on one side and my witnesses
on the other.

In the large crowd, I catch a glimpse of Raffaele's
back; he's seated next to his counsel. His body moves back
as he stands up. I turn my head to avoid his glance. I see
Dan holding Katrina's hand; she squeezes mine.

"You'll get him," Dan whispers.

"All rise. Court is now in session. Justice Lampkin
presiding," the court clerk announces.

The judge seats himself and beckons to the courtroom
to do the same. Lampkin surveys the courtroom, peers over
his bifocals, nods, and begins:

"In this trial, the issue of the old common law is
applicable to try an offender for the breaching of a

probation order, made in Canada, even if the actual breach of it has occurred in Cuba. On May 21, 1999, I have dismissed the motion to stay for reason on May 21, 1999, reported at (1999) 136. CCC (3d) 271, ruling that Mr. Raffaele Grecci be tried, today, for breaching his probation order, while in force, because his probation follows him wherever he goes."

Justice Lampkin pauses for a moment. It's my first time, ever, inside a courtroom. I already feel drained, mostly by the question—why am I putting myself through this? Is it worth doing?

So far, I have learned a way to survive, mentally, in my search for justice; I keep my eyes fixed on my journal to record the proceeding. This exercise keeps my focus. There is always the flip side of the coin.

Mr. Justice Lampkin clears his throat, again.

"Is the Crown counsel ready to present her case before the Queen's court?" he enquires.

The young, petite Crown counsel assistant, Marcy Henschell, stands.

"Yes, Your Lordship, I am," she replies.

"Than shall we begin?"

Immediately, Henschell begins reciting the history of my relationship with the offender.

"Raffaele Grecci met Marisha Manley in June 1998, in the Toronto area. They are both Canadian citizens and residents of Ontario. While they were on a weeklong holiday, Mr. Grecci viciously attacked Ms. Manley."

The noise of reporters writing in their notepads can be heard; everyone else remains silent throughout the recital, until the recount of the attack itself. The Crown counsel states,

"During the last night of their vacation, when Ms. Manley awoke, Mr. Grecci was attacking her, yelling repeatedly that he would kill her."

I can't stand the pain as Marcy Henschell continues.

"Raffaele Grecci held her by her hair and punched her numerous times in the head and face. Ms. Manley was able to escape and ran out of the room without her clothing, screaming for help. A number of Canadian tourists at the resort assisted Ms. Manley. Because of this attack, Ms. Manley suffered severe facial bruising, an open cut of one centimetre to the right cheek, which required stitches, and a fracture of her cheekbone; her nose was deviated and she received a cut to her upper lip. Her injuries required hospital treatment in Cuba and in Canada."

Angry whispers spread throughout the courtroom. His Lordship lifts his head.

"Excuse me, Crown counsel. I have a question," he says. "I understand there are other allegations against Mr. Grecci, besides this assault upon Ms. Manley? Isn't this right?

"Yes, Your Lordship," the Crown counsel assistant responds.

"They need to be observed, at this time," His Lordship says.

"Yes, Your Lordship."

"Please, Ms. Henschell, sit down for a moment as I brief this," Justice Lampkin asks.

Henschell rests, and His Honour continues.

"Mr. Grecci has been examined by Detective Strong of the York Regional Police Department, in which course of this investigation Detective Strong ascertained that Mr. Grecci was on probation in December of 1998 and January of 1999 for uttering threats and assault. On top of that, Mr. Raffaele Grecci also has a criminal record, as follows: March 12, 1982, he was convicted of impaired driving for which he was fined the sum of 1,000 or 20 days' incarceration, in default; September 1, 1982, he was found guilty of possession of a narcotic for which he received a conditional discharge and probation for two years; January 7, 1991, he was convicted for mischief over $1,000 and assault upon a peace officer, for which he received a suspended sentence and probation for one year."

Justice Lampkin looks at the offender. "August 10, 1992, he was convicted of driving with more than 80 milligrams of alcohol in 100 millilitres of blood, for which he was fined the sum of $2,000 or 45 days' incarceration in default; January 18, 1994, he was convicted of mischief over $1,000 for which he was fined a sum of $400 or 8 days' incarceration in default and probation for two years. May 7, 1997, he was convicted of uttering threats and assault for which he was sentenced to time served (13 days) and probation for two years."

The convictions arouse my anger toward his family— for deceiving me and for keeping such an extensive record of his wrongdoings completely hidden.

I get a glimpse of my perpetrator; his hair is now longer than I have ever seen it. He looks ragged, very unattractive; he's shaking his head nervously from side to side, definitely trying to dismiss his criminal record in his mind.

"March 4, 1999, Detective Strong swore information against Mr. Grecci with respect to the present charge," Justice Lampkin says. After a momentary silence, he then resumes, with a stare right at Grecci.

He calls to Henschell, "Please resume your submission."

"Yes, Your Lordship. On behalf of the Crown, I submit that the court does have jurisdiction to try Mr. Raffaele Grecci. He is presently charged with the breach of a probation order made by The Court of Canada, and although the breach is the alleged assault in Cuba, the court in Canada has jurisdiction for the following reasons:

"The probation was made in the province of Ontario. There is a real link with Canada since the victim, the accused, and the witnesses are all Canadians. Cuba has expressed no desire to prosecute Mr. Grecci for the offence of assault. Cuba has no jurisdiction to try Mr. Grecci on a charge of breach of probation. Only a court in Canada has jurisdiction to enforce the terms of a probation order made by the court in Canada. The crime may go unpunished if Canada does not assume jurisdiction. There is no extradition treaty between Canada and Cuba, and if any charge were to be laid against Mr. Grecci in Cuba, he cannot be forced to return to Cuba for his trial but would have to return voluntarily. The criminal record of Mr. Raffaele Grecci and his assault upon the complainant, Ms. Marisha Manley, portray a need to protect the Canadian public from him. The assumption of jurisdiction by a Canadian court does not offend international comity because Cuba has no interest in prosecuting Mr. Grecci. There is a continuing obligation to abide by the terms of a probation order and the requirement to keep the peace remains with the probationer and follows him wherever he goes."

The Crown counsel assistant, Marcy Henschell, closes her folder and then walks quickly back to the prosecutors' table.

Justice Lampkin motions and then speaks.

"I will now ask Marisha Manley to take the stand," he states.

I raise myself from the bench.

"Ms. Marisha Manley, could you please take the stand."

I walk to the front of the courtroom. Everything and everyone becomes a blur. Perhaps this is a subconscious defence mechanism to shield myself from viewing my attacker.

The clerk places a Bible in front of me.

"You're Marisha Manley?" she enquires.

"Yes, I am."

"Please place your right hand on the Bible. Do you swear that everything you say will be the truth, and nothing but the truth?"

"I do."

His Honour clears his voice and commences.

"Before me I have pictures of you, Ms. Manley. However, the person in these photos hardly resembles you. Obviously, the woman in these photos has been brutally beaten. Ms. Manley, I'm told that these photographs of you were taken by Steve Joyce. Is this correct, Ms. Manley?"

"Yes, Your Lordship, they are pictures of me taken by Steve Joyce."

The Justice shakes his head and asks the Crown counsel if she's ready to proceed.

"Yes, I am, Your Lordship," Henschell responds and then immediately begins questioning me.

"Ms. Manley, can you tell the court who assaulted you?"

"Raffaele Grecci," I state.

"When did you first meet him?"

I take a deep breath and clear my throat.

"I met him in Toronto, June of 1998."

"How would you describe your relationship with him?"

My mind races as I'm forced to discuss the intimacies of my relationship in public court.

"Raffaele Grecci and I, we had a loving relationship. He and I loved each other. He treated me well, until I was on vacation with him in Cuba."

"How did you happen to be in Cuba?"

"The vacation was a Christmas gift from Raffaele Grecci."

"What happened in Cuba?"

"The first night, Raffaele Grecci called me disgusting names in public. I left the table and went back to the hotel. He argued with me, and then shoved me into a television in the room, that evening. My leg and ankle were bruised, and I hit my head on the marble floor. I obtained my own suite from the resort management and we stayed separated for a few days after that incident. During that time, Raffaele Grecci approached me several times and asked for

204

forgiveness; we spent time talking the incident out and the day of New Year's we reconciled. On the last day, Raffaele Grecci, after I had fallen asleep, he attacked me."

Cold chills shake my body. I pause, still searching for the reason why he assaulted me. I can't believe that this happened. I can't find any real answer, except that he is a very sick man.

"At what time did this attack occur?" His Lordship questions, forcing me to regain my focus.

"It happened between one and two o'clock in the morning."

"Could you please describe what happened that night?"

I probe my memory of that fateful night.

"I was on my knees. My head was being held up by my hair and a fist was punching me to my right. With every hit, every fist to my face, he said the words, 'I will kill you.'" I teeter, momentarily, then regain my voice. "I escaped to the room of Liza and Steve Joyce." I take a deep breath, looking straight at Raffaele Grecci. I break down in tears. What I had been intending to say for a long time now slips uncontrollably from my mouth, in a scream: "Why? Why? Why did you do this to me?" I'm shocked, yet relieved that I can finally confront him. Tears stream down my cheeks, and I shake irrepressibly.

"Do you need to be excused from the stand?" Justice Lampkin asks.

"Yes, please," I say, sobbing. "It was horrible. I can't keep . . ."

I shake, uncontrollably.

Then, confronting him directly, I cry out loudly,

"Why did you do this to me?"

"You may be excused," Mr. Justice Lampkin repeats.

Alice, the victim assistant, ushers me from the courtroom.

Katrina follows beside me. My tears just keep flowing. My chest is pounding. I'm gasping for air. Katrina cries and hugs me. Alice reaches toward us, wraps my hands in hers, and takes us to the Victim's Room. Alice says,

"Now, the witnesses are called one by one."

Later I learn about their testimonies from the transcripts and the newspaper articles. Laurel Baig was the first one on the stand.

"I went to Cuba for a family vacation from December 21, 1998, to January 4, 1999," she said. "We stayed at the Caribe del Farrallon, the sister hotel to Marre Del Portillo. The two hotels were located approximately 2 miles from each other and were run by the same owners and shared staff and services."

"When did you meet Raffaele Grecci and Marisha Manley?" The Crown counsel Henschell enquired.

"I first noticed Raffaele Grecci and Marisha Manley on the first evening of my holiday, when Raffaele Grecci made some terrible remarks at the table and she left. Then, I saw them on the horseback ride, on Sunday, January 3. Just before the day they were leaving back to Canada, they both looked happy."

"Please, tell the court when you learned of the assault."

"On Sunday morning, when I was giving first aid to a moped accident victim. The hotel staff at the Farrallon informed me that a woman at the Marre Del Portillo had been beaten terribly by her husband and had been taken to the hospital. At that point it was fairly common knowledge that someone had beaten Ms. Marisha Manley. I was told that her skull had been broken."

"Did you see Ms. Marisha Manley at any time after the assault?"

"Yes. On Monday, January 4, 1999, I saw Marisha at the airport and she was covered with bandages. I thought the attacker must have been the man she had been with on Sunday. My suspicions were confirmed when I arrived at the airport waiting area. Some of my friends from the Marre Del Portillo pointed out Raffaele Grecci as the attacker. He was sitting alone. Some members of the group were discussing the incident. Raffaele Grecci approached me and told me it was rude to talk behind somebody's back. I called him a monster, and he answered, 'This is the first time I've ever hit a woman.' Upon arrival at the Toronto airport, I saw Raffaele Grecci talking to the police. I offered this information to the officers. As he was being taken off the plane, I overheard him telling the police that this was the first time he had ever attacked anyone."

"Thank you, Miss Baig," Justice Lampkin says, and pauses. "May we call the next witness, Mr. Steve Joyce, to the stand, please?"

"Mr. Steve Joyce, as I understand from your statement, you and your wife, Liza Joyce, spent quite a bit of time with Marisha Manley and her then-boyfriend,

Raffaele Grecci, at the resort while vacationing in Cuba?"
Justice Lampkin enquires.

"Yes, we did, Your Lordship."

"Crown counsel, please proceed," Justice Lampkin
says, and Henschell resumes.

"Please, could you describe the events occurring
January 3rd, 1999, in Cuba?"

Immediately, Steve Joyce begins:

"It was approximately 12 A.M.; a group of people,
including Marisha and Raffaele, were at the Beach Bar.
Music was playing; Marisha danced a couple of times with
my wife. Then, Marisha and Raffaele left. Shortly after
1:30 A.M., I also decided to retire for the night. I returned to
my room with my wife. I was just going to bed about 2:30
A.M. when there was heavy banging at my door.

"I opened the door and found Marisha, who was very
battered. A light robe was glued to her body with blood,
and her face was covered with blood; she was spitting up
blood. She was in shock, screaming, crying and yelling
that Raffaele Grecci had tried to kill her."

"Mr. Joyce, what did you do at that moment?" the
Crown counsel interjects.

"Fearing that Raffaele was chasing Marisha, I helped
her into our room and locked the door behind her. I called
to my wife to wake up. Liza awoke and we both tried to get
her to sit, but Ms. Manley was falling into a coma. Liza
was holding Marisha. I grabbed a heavy bathrobe, and Liza
wrapped her in it. Marisha was moaning and bleeding
heavily, particularly from the cuts on her face."

"How did help come?" the Crown counsel asked.

"I left Marisha with Liza and ran outside to call security. When I stepped away from my hotel room, I saw a security guard and called for him. He came over, and then I saw Raffaele Grecci at the top of the stairs leading to Marisha's hotel room. He was more concerned about his own injuries than about his girlfriend. He said, 'Thank God, you're here; she attacked me!' I saw no injuries on Raffaele Grecci. I ignored him, told the security guard to remain right outside my door, and went back into my room, where both of my children were now awake. I told my kids to look the other way and that I would explain later.

"Marisha was moaning and now bleeding more heavily. Liza and I took her into the bathroom. She vomited, throwing up blood. We were worried that she might have internal injuries and decided we had better call for more help.

"Leaving the hotel room, with the guard still at my door, I started back to the swimming pool area, where I noticed another security guard. I asked him if he spoke English; he said, 'No, but Ramon, the bartender, does.' I sent him to get Ramon. Seconds later, one of the hotel entertainers, Ariel, who spoke English, came out of the changing room. I yelled out to him and said to come with me. Ariel came back to my room, followed by two more security guards and Ramon.

"When Ariel and Ramon saw Ms. Manley's condition, they said that we needed a doctor. Ramon went back to tend the bar, and Ariel sent one of the guards to get the doctor.

"While waiting for the doctor, Ariel, the two security guards, and I walked down the row of hotel rooms to

Marisha's room to see if we could get her shoes or clothes. Raffaele must have heard us or seen us coming. He came out onto the balcony, asked for a doctor, and yelled, 'I acted in self-defence!' Ariel told him that the doctor was coming, and asked if we could have some clothes and a pair of Marisha's shoes.

"Raffaele threw us a pair of high-heeled dress shoes, which we took back to my room. The shoes didn't seem suitable, so we got a pair of my son's running shoes and got them on her. I took three pictures of Marisha, just quick shots from behind and into the bathroom mirror, while Liza was trying to wash the blood off Marisha's face. We were worried that the doctor was taking too long, so I went to the front desk and inquired as to the delay. Then, we phoned the sister hotel, Farrallon, where the nurse and doctor stayed; they assured me, the nurse was on her way.

"Sure enough, when I returned to my hotel room, the nurse had just arrived. She checked Marisha. Then, she decided that she had better look at Raffaele because he had been complaining that he was hurt, also. The nurse, Ariel, two or three security guards, and I went back to Marisha's hotel room, and Raffaele asked the nurse in.

"There was blood splattered all over the bed, up the wall, the drapes, and across the floor. Raffaele was complaining that he was hurt and asked the nurse to look at his hand, which was now wrapped in a towel. She examined his hand and showed it to Ariel, the guards, and me. Ariel asked Raffaele where the injury was. Raffaele became quite angry with him, apparently for suggesting that there wasn't really any sign of injury. Raffaele demanded a doctor, and the nurse, through Ariel, told him to wait and they would get back to him. We all left the room and returned to my room. The nurse said we would now go to the hospital, so with the help of the guards, we got Marisha into the front seat of a Suzuki Samurai. I thought it would be better if there was a familiar face and language around for Marisha, so I went as well.

"It was a ten- to fifteen-minute drive to the hospital in Pilon. We arrived there, I believe, around 3:45 A.M. We had to wait a bit for the doctor, but when he arrived he agreed to examine Marisha immediately, in the hall, rather than moving her off the gurney. Marisha was complaining of a lot of back and neck pain, and I didn't want her moving any more than necessary. The doctor examined her and cleaned and stitched up the cut on her cheek (two stitches). Then, the doctor decided he wanted X-rays in case there were any broken bones. They took a lot of X-rays, 15 or 20, I think. It was difficult moving Marisha off the gurney as well as her having to roll over on the X-ray table.

"It was while they were taking X-rays that Maria, the Alba Tour representative, arrived. She stayed with Marisha and me the rest of the time at the hospital and translated for the doctors. The nurse also took blood and urine samples.

"Shortly after we arrived at the hospital, Ariel showed up. He had brought Raffaele in another vehicle, apparently because he was demanding X-rays for his hands. I know they took at least two X-rays of his hands because I saw them. Raffaele was examined by the doctor, also, and then was left in another room with a couple of beds and a bathroom. He fell asleep, shortly thereafter.

"Another doctor arrived at the hospital around 5 A.M. I think he was the senior of the two. He examined Marisha and studied the X-rays, and then came in with the first doctor and Maria. The doctor explained through Maria that they were required to notify the police and asked if Marisha would make a statement. Marisha told the doctors that she wanted to charge Raffaele with assault and that she also wanted a full description of the doctor's examination, diagnosis, and test results. They said they would provide that. Maria suggested that Marisha be returned to the hotel and that the police could come and interview her there.

"At approximately 6:15 A.M., Marisha, Maria, the hotel nurse, and I returned to our hotel, arriving at 6:30 A.M. Maria arranged for another hotel room for Marisha, and we all helped her get there. Maria and I and one security guard went back to Marisha's room to get her belongings and move them to her new room. The former room was a mess. I took pictures of the room with Marisha's camera, and then I went back to her new room to take pictures of her there.

"Around 6:50 A.M., I returned to my room and found Liza. I told her what had gone on and then lay down for an hour. I visited Marisha later in the morning, took a few more pictures, and then left her with Liza, Anna Marie, and some other friends. I didn't see Raffaele any more that day; I saw Marisha again at about 3 P.M. as she was leaving for the airport."

"Thank you, Mr. Joyce. You may step down."

The next person asked to testify is Steve's wife, Liza Joyce. Her testimony further reinforces the events of that night, just as her husband, Steve Joyce, had already stated on the stand.

"When I first saw Marisha at our door, she was covered in blood, very battered, screaming that Raffaele Grecci was trying to kill her," she said. "I took care of her. Then, after she was taken to the hospital, I went to the Dinning room, where I saw Raffaele. His knuckles were raw, obviously from hitting someone. He had one small scratch on his hand. That's all. He said he did it in self-defence."

At the end, Liza summed it up.

"It's a real miracle that Marisha is alive today. When I saw her after fleeing her attacker, I knew that a few more blows to her head, and she'd be dead for sure."

I read on from the transcript. Anna Marie Atkins was next to take the stand.

"Can you please describe for the court in your own words your meeting with the defendant, Raffaele Grecci, and the plaintiff, Marisha Manley, during your vacation, in Cuba?" Henschell asked.

"The second day of our holiday at the resort, my husband Mike and I were watching a pig being roasted. We struck up a conversation with Marisha. She mentioned that her back and her hip were bothering her and that her boyfriend had pushed her to the floor the night before. She was very upset."

"When did you see Marisha Manley next?"

"A few days later, Your Lordship. When my husband and I met Marisha at the adjacent hotel, she was with Raffaele then. The four of us got to know each other over lunch. Then, we were together with them during a horseback riding trip and on another excursion to the village, for a lobster dinner."

"Mrs. Atkins, I have some very graphic photos in front of me. Could you please elaborate on how you came to take these pictures that are submitted to this court and marked Evidence Number B11?"

"Your Lordship, Marisha's room looked like the scene of a murder. I thought it was important to take some shots of it with my camera. It was so sad to see a beautiful woman like Marisha barely able to get on the bus to the airport. We confronted Raffaele before he left but, Your Lordship, he showed no remorse or responsibility for his actions. At this point I realized he had a very serious problem."

"Thank you, Mrs. Atkins. You may step down. I call now Cathy Boudrie to the stand."

Cathy's testimony echoed Anna Marie's, reinforcing my gruesome experience even more, and ended with her assisting me on the flight back to Canada. Cathy stepped down and, at this point, Judge Lampkin ordered a fifteen-minute recess.

Dan comes back to the victims and witnesses room and informs us that everyone's testimony is going as planned. He suggests that we go outside for some air. We walk down the hall, but just as we leave the courthouse, I look to my right and a reporter flashes me a sympathetic smile, then returns his eyes to his notepad.

Once outside, the fresh air feels good, until I see him standing smoking a cigarette. Then a few reporters see me and they snap into action.

"Can I ask you a question?" one of the reporters asks. "What would you like to have happen today in court?"

"I believe that even though I'm unable to charge Raffaele Grecci in Canada for the crime he committed against me in Cuba, I hope that he'll be charged, at least for his breach of probation."

We walk back down the long hall.

"Don't look to your left," Liza whispers. "For some reason, Raffaele is loitering just ahead in the hall."

"Yes. He's with his defence lawyer."

We return to the courtroom. Justice Lampkin announces,

"The trial resumes tomorrow at 10 A.M."

It's a long night before the morning comes. The first person I see is him walking into the courthouse, and smiling. Surely, he can't think that the case is going in his favour.

Justice Lampkin clears his voice and looks sternly toward Raffaele and his defence lawyer. His Lordship commences,

"I now ask Mr. Raffaele Grecci to take the stand. I'm about to ask you a series of questions, sir, very important questions, and I want you to respond to them honestly. If you fail to respond, I'll regard it as contempt of court. Do you, Raffaele Grecci, understand that the physical component, *actus reus*, (the guilty act), that you have committed against Marisha Manley involved a brutal assault?"

"I acted in self-defence," he replies.

My heart stops. Good God! He's lying, again. What does he think he's accomplishing by this perpetual denial?

215

"Mr. Grecci, yesterday a witness, Laurel Baig, testified that after Ms. Marisha Manley was assaulted, you confirmed that fact at the airport. Mr. Grecci, you said to Ms. Baig that this was the first time you had ever beaten a woman," Justice Lampkin momentarily pauses. "Mr. Grecci," he says, "I remind you that you're still under oath. Your past record shows an assault on your ex-wife, Gabriella Grecci. And, surely, you can't deny assaulting Ms. Marisha Manley? The injuries showing in these photos from Cuba prove that Ms. Marisha Manley has been violently assaulted. The photos of the room where the assault occurred reveal the brutality of this assault. The testimonies of witnesses Mr. Steve and Mrs. Liza Joyce, Ms. Boudrie, and Mrs. Atkins verify that you have assaulted Ms. Manley. Detective Strong, who interviewed the Cuban doctor, who examined Ms. Manley in Cuba after the assault, confirms this evidence. The doctor documented Ms. Manley's injuries as being a fractured nose and cheek, a split lip and black eye, and a cut under her right eye." Mr. Justice Lampkin pauses. "Mr. Grecci, do you understand that by lying you are in contempt of court? Do you really want to add that to your current charges?"

"No, I don't, but there's no law for you to convict me, here in Canada." he answers, angrily.

His Lordship sinks back into his chair, closes his eyes, and then rubs them intensely.

"Mr. Grecci, this assault was very serious," His Honour states firmly.

"Sorry, Judge. Let me explain it again. There's no law for me to be charged in Canada."

"No further questions, Mr. Grecci; you're excused."
His Honour pauses, looks sternly at the defendant and his
counsel, and closes a file before him, adding,
    "Court adjourned for trial. I reserve judgment till
November."
    Katrina squeezes my hand; Dan looks over with a half
smile. Everyone around me hugs me, in what I hope will
become a victory celebration. Court artists and cameras are
already eager to report my comments for their newspapers.
They follow us toward the revolving doors. Outside the
courthouse, the questions begin.
    "What do you think the courts should do, in your
case?" the *Toronto Star* reporter asks.
    I think for a moment, before I answer.
    "The justice system must amend a jurisdictional law
for Canadian victims, enabling them to charge the crime
committed against them by another Canadian in countries
with which Canada does not have a treaty, such as Cuba." I
run out of breath; I pause, but I need to say more, so I take
a deep breath and continue. "In my case, the courts can
only prosecute the offender on the basis of his breach of
probation. This in fact omits the crime done to me."
    We walk quickly away, so as not to break down in
front of the cameras, toward the cars. Liza, Steve, and Anna
Marie are huddling. Laurel is standing beside Detective
Strong.
    Liza takes out a cigarette and lights it.
    "It's incredible," she says. She takes another puff of
her cigarette, inhales fiercely, and continues,
    "So much work, Marisha, for such a small victory.
And, we still don't know if he'll get charged, at all."

We know that she's right. The conversation lags, everyone looks tired, and a deathly silence hovers over us. There's nothing left to be said.

Detective Strong departs and we decide to meet at a restaurant across the street from the courthouse. I'm determined to keep the conversation away from the case. The others seem to follow my lead.

An hour later, sitting in my psychologist's office, I explain,

"We tried to have lunch; however, peace did not last for long," I stutter in panic.

"What happened, Marisha?" she asks and hands me a Kleenex.

"As the food was being brought, Liza headed for the restroom. When she returned, her face was paler than a ghost. She blurted out, 'I saw him! He's there! He's sitting at the bar, in the side room!'"

"Of course, it's one thing to see him at the courthouse, but in a private place you would be terrified, no doubt!" she empathizes, and then asks, "So what happened?"

"I panicked and everyone left the restaurant, as fast as we could."

"I was going straight home; however, Katrina brought me here. I feel traumatized, again." I grit my teeth and grip the sides of my chair.

"Marisha, you have had enough of this trauma. Hopefully, he'll be charged soon!"

I can't add anything else.

Chapter 20. Small Victory for a Brutal Crime

Whatever was left of the colourful autumn is now replaced by the leaden sky of November. I'm intimidated again, this morning by another, "Court is in session. All rise," which the court clerk announces.

Once again, Justice Lampkin expands on his earlier decision of May 21, 1999.

"Ladies and gentlemen, silence please." He dramatically looks from left to right for the respectful attention of the court.

A hush falls over the courtroom; His Lordship begins delivering a strong lecture on civic responsibility.

"Ordinarily, a citizen who is not subject to the terms of a probation order need only observe the laws of a foreign country where he happens to be. A citizen in a foreign country who is obliged to observe the terms of a probation order has a double obligation."

The offender's body moves forward; he seems eager to blurt out a premature defence. His Honour stares at the defender and states,

"All citizens must observe the laws of the country, wherever they happen to be, and comply with the terms of a probation order. In this case, Raffaele Grecci has brutally assaulted Miss Manley, in Cuba; then, under the laws of

219

Canada, he is accountable for the breach of his probation, in Canada."

The courtroom is silently waiting for the rest of His Honour's judgment.

"Every Canadian is under a common law to keep the peace and be of good behaviour, at home and abroad," His Honour Justice Lampkin adds, taking a sip of water. He then looks across the crowd,

"I have decided that Raffaele Grecci has breached his probation order, which was issued after Raffaele Grecci was convicted of assaulting his ex-wife in 1999. Among other things, he was to keep the peace and be of good behaviour, while abroad and in Cuba, as well as in Canada. The vicious assault Raffaele Grecci has committed against Ms. Manley in Cuba has jurisdiction in Canada."

I notice to the far left my attacker is rocking back and forth, like a truant child, as His Lordship Lampkin stares at Grecci, and maintains,

"I charge you, Raffaele Grecci, on or about the 4th day of January 1999, in the country of Cuba, while bound by a probation order made by the Provincial Court of the Regional Municipality of Peel, on the 7th day of May 1997, you have failed, without reasonable excuse, to comply with the said order, to wit, to keep the peace and be of good behaviour, contrary to s.733.1 (1) of the *Criminal Code of Canada.*"

At least Grecci's probation order continues to be against him! At least a bit of justice to keep this criminal away from me!

"And, to account for this offence, I sentence you, Raffaele Grecci, to a term of nine months in prison, and two years probation, And, in all fairness I will reiterate, if this assault had occurred in Canada, you are well aware that you'd be serving up to fourteen years, sir. Because there's no provision in the *Criminal Code* for your crime, I'm sorry that I can incarcerate you only for this far too short a term."

Twenty yards down the hallway, the police take Grecci into custody. The courtroom crowd, witnesses, and well-wishers are all smiling with exuberance. My daughter, Katrina, is the first to speak,

"You did it, mom!" Tears fill her eyes. She throws her arms around my neck and Dan joins in the hug.

A TV reporter stops us, and asks,

"Miss Manley, can you comment on your victory, today? Your case is precedent-setting."

I ponder his question for a moment, nodding, as I try to find the best way to express with honesty, how I truly feel.

"Yes, I'm happy about Judge Lampkin's ruling," I state, then pause to speak the truth. "Otherwise, the perpetrator would never have been punished at all for his crime against me. I'm definitely relieved that some justice has been served." However, the little voice inside me cries, *The crime done against me by Raffaele Grecci has not truly been vindicated.*

We walk to the parking lot; the word "victory" still sounds hollow to me.

"Oh, Marisha," Liza says. "You have come such a long, long way for so little justice, sweetie."

"It's been a nightmare, Liza." I say, and I'm thinking that something positive must come out of this ordeal.

Hopefully, all this attention, all the press, surely will educate the public to push through an amendment to procure a jurisdictional law to the *Canadian Criminal Code*.

The next day brings more media coverage. This time, three separate newspapers carry a report on my case.

The *Toronto Star* heralds in bold print:
Man convicted of breaching probation for attack in Cuba—"Justice has been served," says his ex-girlfriend.
"Yes, I am relieved to a degree," the writer quotes my statement in the article, and then continues:
A Newmarket judge has convicted a Toronto man for breaching a Canadian probation order when he viciously beat a woman in Cuba this year.
I suppose that some justice is better than none. I purse my lips as I read on, until the third paragraph, where the reporter concludes,
This case is unusual because it's believed to be the first time a citizen of this country has been convicted here for an offence relating to an incident that took place outside Canada.
Yes, my case is unusual, but for a democratic country like Canada not to punish a criminal? I could understand if I lived in a primitive land, where there were no laws, but here in Canada not to receive justice? It's a disgrace!

I go on to the second article, in the *Globe and Mail*:
Man jailed for assault in Cuba—Attack on woman breached Canadian probation order.

What victory? The precedent-setting ruling still appears to me as a drop in the legal bucket to convict Grecci only on the basis of probation (Grecci's crime upon his ex-wife). I am not vindicated! What about setting a precedent to charge the crime itself? I shake the newspaper: I know that the road will be long. I'm determined it will be uphill, and I continue reading the report, seeing that he sheds light upon my very concern that:

There is no law under the Canadian Criminal Code *to prosecute a Canadian's crime committed on foreign soil.*

I nod in agreement as I read on.

Grecci's lawyer, Frank Snow, argues that the probation order does not require his client to keep the peace in another country.

I shudder to think that if Grecci's criminal lawyer had argued his point successfully, his client would have walked.

The third article appears in *The Toronto Sun:*

Prison time too good for coward.

The Sun has no sympathy for Grecci, as they deem him, *a repulsive habitual woman-beating monster! He, certainly, knew what he was doing.*

The reporter further expounds,

It is not often that you leave a criminal court with the grim satisfaction that justice has been done. But yesterday was one of those days, and it was deeply gratifying to hear the soft click of the handcuffs as they encircled the wrists of wife-beater Raffaele Grecci. It's not as if this man with the unkempt hair and the mean, thin mouth didn't know what was coming. His lawyer conceded as much in his sentencing submissions when he acknowledged that the judge was likely going to impose a jail term of more than 30 days. And although Grecci's counsel tried to delay the inevitable by asking for an adjournment until next week, Judge Vibert A. Lampkin was having none of it. In a pithy ruling that dripped with revulsion for Grecci's latest crime, Lampkin opened by noting the wiry 36-year-old salesman had assaulted a sleeping woman.

I consider the further words of the reporter, who again quotes Judge Lampkin in court:

"If you want to attack someone, put on some gloves and get into the ring and let them beat your brains out," he *told Grecci with embittered contempt. "You don't attack a sleeping person. It is worst than kicking a dog."*

The newspaper reporter sees reality, and so will the readers. I believe it is a small step forward: increasing public awareness to the need for amending this legal loophole.

The psychologist continues to counsel me on how to handle these continuous court sessions, all the newspaper exposure, and the public discussions of my case.

"The strange turn of events in my life has become even more unusual than my case, itself. The newspaper articles have made me the centre of public attention; the alarming news affects my life, everywhere I go."

"Yes, in a teaching profession you're in the public eye, as it is," she sympathizes.

"My students are happy that there's a small victory. The petition to amend the law is under review, but the court sessions wear me down. And so what if my case is precedent-setting for all Canadians; everyone is still confused."

"I know what you mean," she empathizes.

"My students ask me, 'Miss, what's up with the law?'"

"This must be so difficult for you, Marisha," she nods.

"Everyone knows that the crime committed against me has been vindicated. They continue to ask me questions for which I have no answer. It breaks my heart when they say, 'Miss, our families travel to Cuba often. How can we be protected if something like this happens to us on holiday?'"

"Hopefully, the justice system will do something about the law soon and you'll be absolved," she states.

It makes sense that, during the next school assembly, my principal suggests that I give the students some clarification of what has exactly happened with my court case. Many questions fly from the students. They ask,

"Miss, how did your case become precedent-setting?"

However, the senior grades that I teach are more concerned that the crime committed against me has not been vindicated. They ask,

"Why wasn't the actual crime ever charged?"

The students are unashamed to say that the crime executed against me has not been charged. In fact, they say,

"It's a crime of the justice system that the crime carried out against you, Miss Manley, has only been submitted to the Supreme Court of Canada because of another violent crime that he perpetrated upon his ex-wife, few years ago."

The students stop me in the hallways later on and demand even more explanation.

"Miss, are you going to get this law amended?" many of them ask.

"I honestly hope so!" I tell them, wishing that I could give them a more positive answer.

For months, I receive phone calls from petitioners for which I am ever so grateful. This particular one has been checking in with me occasionally. She asks me,

"Can the judicial system rest and morally believe that justice has been served in your case? Do they in their wildest bureaucratic dreams believe that using your name in the precedent-setting—this small bone of justice thrown in your direction—is enough to buy citizens' complacency?"

At this point, I can only answer,

"I look upon all God's graces and am thankful for people like you and the media who all have stimulated public awareness and opinion."

"More and more people will continue to question the lack of a law to protect Canadians abroad and support you in your quest to carry the judicial battle until the law gets amended," she concludes.

Chapter 21. Plea to Petitions Disposed!

Winter. Fresh, glistening snow lies heaped on either side of my driveway. Before closing the front door, I reach into my full mailbox in anticipation of Christmas cards or greetings for a "better New Year." They are there, but also something else, which makes me sweat in the cold: a foreboding business envelope with a seal from The House of Commons.

"Oh, great! It's the response from the Minister of Justice!" I say aloud. My heartbeat speeds up. I wonder if the petition was accepted positively.

I enter my home and rip open the brown envelope. I speed-read the two-page cover letter.

"Where is the word, "AMENDMENT"?" I ask myself, loudly.

"Perhaps I missed it," I say to myself.

With my coat still on, I sit down at the living-room table and continue reading aloud every single word:

RESPONSE TO PETITIONS—by the Minister of Justice and Attorney General of Canada—Subject Criminal Code of Canada.

The petition proposes that the Criminal Code *be amended to enable the victims of crime to lay criminal charges in Canada when a serious criminal offence takes place outside Canada and when both of the parties have Canadian status.*

My hopes are dashed!

"Brilliant," I say. "This *is* my very petition, but where is the actual response?"

I'm flabbergasted. How can the Minister of Justice have the audacity to send me a form response? The Minister of Justice is only restating my struggles! As I continue reading the print, I begin to feel as if the Minister of Justice is actually here, sounding out the existing law:

Nationality, as a mark of allegiance and an aspect of sovereignty, is recognized in international law, but more particularly with civil law states, as a basis for jurisdiction over extra-territorial acts.

I can't believe that the Minister of Justice did not understand that this existing section of the *Canadian Criminal Code* is my very reason for petitioning to amend a jurisdictional law within the *Canadian Criminal Code*. I have heard and read this part of the law many times. It's even more obvious in the next body of the print, which cites the actual loophole in the existing law:

However, similar to other common law countries Canada is generally reluctant to use the nationality principle in international law to exert jurisdiction over its citizens for acts or omissions committed outside Canada, except in accord with international agreement or consensus.

This is why the crime done against me goes unpunished? Is it okay with you, Minister of Justice? The crime committed against me, a common Canadian citizen, is unresolved! Is this justice for me and the rest of Canadian population, dear Minister of Justice?

Still sitting with my coat on, I turn to the next paragraph on page two:

Canada primarily bases its jurisdiction on territoriality principle. Subsection 6(2) of the Criminal Code *provides that the provisions of the* Criminal Code *do not apply to offences committed outside Canada, unless otherwise provided by legislation. The territoriality principle is the most substantial basis for states to claim criminal jurisdiction because, among other things, it accords with the sovereignty principle.*

Now is the time to tell me something that I don't know, Minister of Justice. Didn't the brutal crime against me, the voice of the media, and the signatures of 3,000 Canadian citizens provide enough support for you to take the petitions more seriously? How many more victims need to suffer further to make the Canadian peoples' petition relevant? How I hoped that the Minister of Justice would walk a mile in my shoes.

The next section in the form response is an excerpt of the law which claims that there are exceptions to the law for those who fall under the categories of *aircraft hijacking, hostage taking, protection of nuclear materials, torture, war crime, and piracy,* and for government officials.

"Well," I say to myself. "Of course I have been tortured abroad! Isn't that so, Minister of Justice? I guess as a mere Canadian citizen, I'm not important enough for my country to provide me with basic justice since my perpetrator is also a private Canadian citizen. In my case, I have no right to this exception of the law. However, if a Cuban official had assaulted me, I would have diplomatic possibilities to pursue justice!"

I resume reading the rest of the petition response, which seems to be basically a convoluted explanation of a ridiculous loophole.

Then the last sentence fills me even more with grief and despair:

Any need to extend the scope of Canadian criminal jurisdiction will be carefully studied on a case by case basis, bearing in mind the general principle of international law.

In my case the Canadian criminal jurisdiction has been applied in courts, and the only possibility in which the Canadian justice system was able to apply was to Grecci's probations. No likelihood of amending the law. Thanks, dear Minister, for protecting us all!

On February 9, 2000, media coverage continues. Justice R. Mackey upholds Justice Lampkin's conviction and dismisses Grecci's appeals. Monday February 15, 2000, the *Toronto Star* prints:

Probation Sentence Upheld

An appeals court last week upheld the jailing of a Toronto man who violated his Canadian probation order by savagely beating his then-girlfriend, while on vacation at a Cuban resort in 1999. On appeal, Raffaele Grecci's lawyer argued the jurisdiction belongs to Cuba. But Justice R. MacKinnon of the Superior Court of Justice upheld the nine-month sentence, saying, "Canada has a legitimate interest in prosecuting the probation breach."

"At least some justice," I say to all concerned.

However, my elation is short-lived. The following day, Detective Strong notifies me that Grecci's lawyer is questioning Justice R. MacKinnon's ruling and lodges yet another appeal, this time to another judge, Mr. Justice Finlayson.

Now, I can only hope that Justice Finlayson will not overturn Grecci's conviction and sentence. A few days pass. Detective Strong, wearing a long face, hand-delivers Mr. Justice Finlayson's decision:

ONTARIO COURT OF APPEAL
THE HONOURABLE MR. JUSTICE FINLAYSON
THURSDAY the 15th DAY OF FEBRUARY, A.D. 2000
IN CHAMBERS
IN THE MATTER OF RAFFAELE GRECCI
Convicted and sentenced at the Osgoode Hall
On the 22nd day of November, 1999, and the 2nd day of
December, 1999, respectively, by the Honourable
Mr. Justice Lampkin, for Breach of Probation.

IN THE MATTER OF the appeal of RAFFAELE
GRECCI against the order of the Honourable
Mr. Justice MacKinnon, made on the 9th day of
February, 2000, wherein he dismissed the appeal
against conviction and sentence;

AND NOW AN INMATE at Toronto West Detection Centre;
UPON THE APPLICATION OF THE ABOVE named appellant, Raffaele Grecci, on hearing counsel for the appellant and counsel for the Crown, and upon having read the Notice of Appeal,

IT IS ORDERED that the said appellant, Raffaele Grecci, upon entering into a recognizance in the amount of $2,000.00, with one or more sureties (including Julio Grecci and Gina Mundas) and without deposit be admitted to bail upon fifteen conditions."

1) SURRENDER into custody at the institution from which released by 6:00 p.m.
on the day prior to the hearing of the appeal or on the 15th of August 2001,
whichever is earlier."

"It's not hard to comprehend Justice Finlayson's reason for making such a decision. It's simple. Just like the Minister of Justice has given me in her response," Ruth reiterates over dinner with us.

"Canada primarily bases its jurisdiction on territoriality principal. Subsection 6(2) of the *Criminal Code* provides that the provisions of the *Criminal Code* do not apply to offences committed outside Canada, unless otherwise provided by legislation, even on the breach of probation," I add with anger surging, again.

"Marisha, his father and sister bail him and stand by a criminal!"

"Now I know why his parents and sisters have never told me the truth about him. They have previously stood by his crimes and they do now!" I add.

"More than that, it's unimaginable that Grecci, with a long criminal record, is beyond reproach and the courts are doing nothing!"

"Ruthie, my case may have set a precedent in Canadian courts only for a mere breach of probation. Now even that small victory goes out the window. The bottom line still remains—Grecci is again out on bail!"

I was once warned, "Be prepared for long waits between court sessions." Was that person right! The wait is not weeks, but months and years. Finally, at the end of March, I receive a call from the new Crown counsel, Gillian Roberts, informing me about the criminal trial.

"It's scheduled for this-coming July, in the Supreme Court of Canada, at Queens Park," Gillian cheerfully states. "I will let you know exactly what date as the day approaches."

Chapter 22. The Three Wise Justices

After five months in a holding pattern, July 10, 2001, finally arrives!

Detective Strong leads me down the center aisle of the packed courtroom. We sit in the first row on the right side behind the Crown counsels.

The Crown counsel, Gillian Roberts will apply historical cases to argue that jurisdiction does exist to prosecute Raffaele Grecci.

"All rise," the court clerk announces.

Justice Doherty, a distinguished senior gentleman, is seated between two younger colleagues, Justice Rosenberg and Justice Moldaver: the three wise men on the bench. The paperwork flies between Justice Moldaver, Justice Doherty, Justice Rosenberg, and the clerk. Justice Moldaver adjusts his robe, shuffles through the papers, and raises his voice enough to demand everyone's attention.

"I trust we can proceed with the trial," His Justice Doherty announces. Silence fills the courtroom, except for the sound of the court clerk, who's still browsing through a file. Midway through a stack, she points to some tagged evidence. Justice Moldaver acknowledges it, and asks,

"Is the Crown counsel ready?"

Gillian Roberts quickly rises.

"Yes, Your Lordships."

His Lordship Doherty looks in Grecci's direction and requests,

"Is the defence ready to proceed?"

"Ready, Your Lordship," a middle-aged man in a legal robe responds, brushing back an errant strand of his curly hair.

"Then, shall we proceed."

"Your Lordships, I will elaborate on the issue of the application for why Mr. Raffaele Grecci should be charged for the breach of his probation in Canada." Roberts pauses and then reinstates, "The Crown takes the position that Mr. Raffaele Grecci's probation order issued by Ontario Court of Justice, on May 7, 1997, for assault and threatening death continued to apply to the appellant during his holiday in Cuba. Accordingly, Section 733.1(2) of the *Canadian Criminal Code* required that Mr. Grecci keep the peace and be of good behaviour, wherever in the world he went. Your Lordship."

Then, Crown counsel Roberts submits applications of case upon case: First, she brings forth the case of *R. v. Libman* (1985), 21 C.C.C. (3d) 206 (S.C.C.) *(Tab 1)*. In *Libman*, under the direction of the accused, sales personnel contacted United States residents and attempted to induce them to purchase shares in a corporation in Costa Rica. Misrepresentations were made to potential purchasers by the sales personnel. The court found that only the inducements originated in Canada. The moneys were sent from the United States to Costa Rica or Panama, where they were received. The deprivation was completed in the United States or at the latest in Costa Rica or Panama.

The Crown counsel continues.

"Your Lordship, while factually dissimilar from the *Grecci* case, the general principles set out in *Libman* govern any analysis of jurisdiction. *Libman* specifically rejected the approach of finding a single *situs* of a crime by locating where the gist of a crime occurred, or was completed, (p. 321) Your Lordship. A rigid approach was rejected and the Supreme Court found that an offence can be 'committed' in more than one country. In ruling that Canada had jurisdiction to try the matter, Justice La Forest set out the general test for jurisdiction on p. 232. I might summarize my approach to the limits of territoriality in this way."

Then, Roberts elaborates,

"Your Lordship, as I see it, all that is necessary to make an offence subject to the jurisdiction of our courts is that a significant portion of the activities constituting the offence take place in Canada. As it is put by modern academics, it is sufficient that there be a 'real and substantial link' between an offence and this country."

"Your Lordships, Justice La Forest did not elaborate on what may constitute a real and substantial link. However, he did state that the outer limits of jurisdiction might be coterminous with the requirements of international comity. To clarify these principles, Your Lordship, States ordinarily have little interest in prohibiting activities that occur abroad, and States are hesitant to incur the displeasure of other States by indiscriminate attempts to control activities that take place wholly within the boundaries of those other countries. But there will be cases where Canada has a legitimate interest in prosecuting persons for activities that take place abroad, but have an unlawful consequence in Canada. La Forest stated: 'The protection of the public in this country is widely acknowledged to be a legitimate purpose of criminal law.'"

The Crown counsel, Roberts, brings further application,

"In the current case, Your Lordship, clearly given the prior criminal convictions of Mr. Grecci for violence, and the expressed concern of the probation office that Mr. Grecci becomes violent when he drinks, the public of Canada, including Ms. Manley, is in need of protection. A prosecution, which were to proceed, aimed at protecting the Canadian public advances a legitimate purpose of the criminal law."

Now, Grecci's defence raises himself and asks the court if he can proceed with his client, Grecci's defence.

"My client, Mr. Raffaele Grecci, is innocent of a breach of probation. Canada has no jurisdiction to anchor a criminal offence because the offence occurred in Cuba."

Justice Doherty appears irritated; he rolls his pen in his large fingers and adjourns the court to a later, as yet undetermined, date. This could be six or more months down the road!

This time no news will appear in the paper until the Justices reach a decision.

Many months later, I enter the Osgoode Hall courthouse with Detective Strong by my side. The designated room for the impending trial is on the main floor. The highly buffed and waxed marble floors lead to hallways decorated with heavily ornamented antique fixtures and furnishings. Paintings and sculptures depicting classical images of justice hang along the freshly painted white walls. It all looks so stable, so dependable, so reassuring to me.

"Marisha, this is Jacqueline Cotter." Strong gestures toward a woman sitting behind a small antique desk.

"She's also a permanent fixture of these hallowed halls."

She rises and extends her firm, chubby hand.

"My pleasure, Marisha." She gives me a long, sympathetic look. "Detective Strong has spoken of you. Good luck, today. You truly deserve it!"

My heart warms a bit as I realize here's another soul in my corner pulling for me.

"Another day, another trial, eh, Jacqueline? Lord knows, you've seen them all," Strong says light-heartedly, as he steers me down the main hallway to the waiting room.

As we enter, the bright morning sun pours through four elongated windows in the atrium. Before me looms a familiar oil painting, the blindfolded Lady holding the Scales of Justice. I have seen it before, among other great works of art, but this time, the image does not stir my artist's soul, but rather cuts me to the quick. Now, observing these scales held so reverently, I realize how frivolously and easily they can be tipped in the wrong direction.

"Are you feeling okay, Marisha? You look pale." Detective Strong awakens me from my trance.

"Just a little bit sad, detective. I have not had the time to paint lately."

We sit down on one of the benches that are stretched along the outer walls and down the middle of the atrium.

The antique clock shows ten minutes before nine. From my vantage point, I can see the crowds begin to gather in the long hallway leading to the courtroom. From the corner of my eye, I see Grecci skulking toward the courtroom with a new criminal lawyer by his side. I wonder what happened to the last one. With a metallic gong, the clock strikes nine. I'm already tired as I hear the same old words of the bailiff announcing,

"Court is in session!"

The massive doors open for us to enter. My stomach is doing flip-flops. My eyes lock on the three Crown counsels seated at the front.

Strong ushers me in and sits down beside me. A smattering of court spectators are observing us as I watch my cowardly nemesis, the man who dragged me down into this pit of inequity, move inconspicuously to the front row, with a new woman at his side. She's blond, natural looking, and moves energetically. I wonder what story he and his family have given her.

The sound of the wooden gavel striking the marble block echoes throughout the courtroom.

"All rise! Court will come to order," the bailiff states.

His Lordship Doherty, followed by two younger Justices, Moldaver and Rosenberg, enter from chambers to preside in this Supreme Court. His Lordship Justice Doherty seats himself first.

"Good morning," he says, and motions to the rest of the courtroom. "Quiet, please."

The Crown counsel, Gillian Roberts, is first to restate why Grecci did not comply with his probation order, to keep the peace and be of good behaviour, contrary to the *Criminal Code of Canada.*

Detective Strong, looking at Grecci and his defence, says under his breath,

"Those two look like as if they've been taking dance lessons together."

"I wonder if they could come up with a new routine, today?" I say to myself.

"Sir, I trust you have read the decision by Justice Lampkin of November 22, or you have not done your homework," His Lordship Doherty addresses Grecci's counsel. "It clearly states, 'the probation order, while it's in force, follows the probationer, wherever he goes, and the breach of the term of the probation order, by committing an offence under the law of Canada, is answerable for that breach, in Canada!'"

"Mr. Jensen," Justice Rosenberg continues, his voice a decibel louder. "How can a person commit this crime and have the audacity to think that he could commit the same crime, somewhere else?"

"But . . . Your Lordship," the defence counsel says, "because there is no law or a clear indication that this offence, because of the jurisdiction, is truly a breach of probation. It needs to be charged on the offence, and not on the breach of probation."

Justice Doherty leans forward and loudly intervenes.

"Sir, whether an offence is committed outside of Canada, all that is necessary is that the significant portion of the activities of the offence take place in Canada. This case is a blatant breach of probation!"

240

Defence looks down at his notepad, and then raises his eyes from the page.

"Committed means? Your Lordship, does not the commission of offence lie upon the jurisdiction issued?"

Justice Rosenberg, silent till now, reiterates sternly what his colleges have decided.

"Territorial mal factor of the original probation order spells out, clearly, that there is jurisdiction! And, why would Cuba take the responsibility for one Canadian tourist committing a crime upon another Canadian tourist, when their prisons are already full?"

"But . . . but . . . but . . . Your Lordship! We must look on jurisdiction as a policy."

"We look at these cases, case by case, on the facts in each case," Justice Rosenberg states.

"But we look on the issue if there is a jurisdiction to change the probation," the defence explains.

"Do we look at these cases, one by one, or how you suggest we do look at them?" Justice Doherty asks.

"Your Lordship, if we look on Probation Code Section 733.1 . . ." He stops on these words and Justice Rosenberg intervenes:

"We're well aware of Section 733.1, sir."

"Can you commit an offence in two different provinces?" Justice Moldaver adds.

Grecci's defence scrambles through his papers.

"But! Your Lordship! I stand on 733.1 jurisdiction," he demands.

The three Justices are annoyed; Justice Doherty states,

"Sir, your argument is not helpful to this situation because you can commit the same crime in two different provinces."

Defence continues to argue.

"But, Your Lordship. There's no provision for an international jurisdiction."

"Mr. Jensen! Are you saying, that there's no jurisdiction?" Justice Doherty asks.

"Your Lordship, I quote 733.1 subsection 2." He looks down on his pad and reads,

"Territorial jurisdiction is set in the law except of the international jurisdiction. International jurisdiction allows you to prosecute passport crimes. Your Lordship, Mr. Grecci cannot be charged with breaching a Canadian law because Canadian laws do not apply in Cuba. He did not breach probation because he was not on probation in Cuba."

Justice Doherty, frail in body, yet strong in voice, states,

"I'm inclined to agree with my esteemed colleagues. I do not think that because of international jurisdiction that this crime cannot be charged within a Canadian jurisdiction."

Then Justice Rosenberg says,

"Mr. Jensen, where do you get off, believing that you can travel south of the border to commit a crime, while on probation? When you think it is, legally, inappropriate to argue the jurisdiction!"

Next Justice Moldaver asks,

"In order to accomplish and to give the court the jurisdiction, if the law says, 'thou shall not drink alcohol,' then how do we comply with that law?"

The defence does not respond.

Justice Doherty pulls on his chin.

"Mr. Jensen, you could not know until the case is over, if you insist on arguing jurisdiction." He pauses in silence for a second, then he resumes. "Please, Mr. Jensen, let us review the circumstances. Your client attacked his pregnant wife and nearly murdered Miss Manley. And, what about the protection of the public, in general, sir?"

The Crown counsel Roberts stands up.

"This heinous crime will go unpunished if this man is not convicted in Canada," she contends.

Justice Doherty nods to Roberts; she pauses, then he returns to addressing the defence.

"Is it a breach by an order of probation to satisfy Section 6? Canada has a jurisdictional application to charge Mr. Grecci for a breach of probation."

The defence sits down and stares at the papers on the table. Grecci looks worried. The Crown counsel, Roberts, is already positioned to speak.

"Your Lordships, in this case, the fact that probation was breached is irrelevant to any other fact."

Grecci is shifting in his seat.

"Yes! Thank you, Crown," Justice Doherty replies. Roberts resumes.

"I can argue that Canadian court would not have any protection if the convicted offender, repeatedly, perpetrated the same crime, over and over."

"Again, on the issue of the act itself, we need to judge, case by case," Justice Doherty reaffirms.

Justice Doherty states,

"Court adjourned until one o'clock in the afternoon."

Strong and I move away from the Osgoode Courthouse and turn south. Sirens blare in the distance, and cars blow their horns, orchestrating a typical downtown business day. The noise irritates me, however. I'm glad for a lunch on a patio on a sunny side of the street.

The Crown counsel Gillian Roberts is the first one to stand up, this afternoon.

"Clearly, there are three aspects to be discussed here. To test the territorial jurisdiction, we need to look at cases similar in many respects to this one. For example, in the case of *R. v. Quellette*, the accused was successfully prosecuted in Canada for manslaughter, as a result of striking his girlfriend, while they were on holiday in the Dominican Republic. The Quebec Supreme Court did not look to see where the wrongful act causing death occurred, but whether there was a real and substantial link to Canada in all the circumstances of the case."

The defence jumps up.

"Your Lordship," he says. "I researched the word 'commit.' It means 'perpetuate or perform, as in an act.' In a bad sense, to commit adultery, fornication: the word 'commit' has a bad connotation. The act itself means the conduct that leads to the commitment of that despicable act." He pauses, looks at his notepad, and repeats his redundant argument, "The *Criminal Code* has no provision of jurisdiction to convict my client of a breach of probation." He sits down.

The Crown counsel Roberts continues.

"Your Lordship, may I please?"

His Lordship Justice Doherty motions to the courtroom and bows his head.

"Please go on," he says.

"The broad contextual approach to territorial jurisdiction set out in this case is appropriate in light of the increasing mobility of peoples and the globalization of criminal activity."

Senior Justice Doherty, holding the law book high in his hands, reaffirms Crown counsel Roberts' premise.

"Yes! And, in this case Mr. Grecci's probation order was established in Canada."

"But, Your Lordship, only with some stipulations," defence Jensen interrupts.

"Mr. Jensen, are you implying that the probation order does not apply to this case? Is this what you're saying?" Justice Rosenberg asks.

Jensen continues to argue.

"He could have been in the United States. He could have been without the probation; then, there would be no act; then, there would be no authority—no enforcement."

"Whatever that person does in the United States, you mean, here in Canada, we don't have authority or enforcement over that violent crime?" Justice Doherty observes the defence.

The defence has no reply.

I'm thinking that I have to appeal, again, to the Minister of Justice. Detective Strong looks down at my notepad; I look up at him; he smiles, and I return to my documenting.

There's no reason for anyone in Canada to suffer as I have! After all, the U.S. has a jurisdictional provision! Then, why won't Canada assume the responsibility for its citizens, especially if there isn't an established international criminal court to prosecute a jurisdictional crime, like this one!

I look up and hear the defence now responding.

"Your Lordship, Canada does not have the authority or enforcement to prosecute my client for a breach of probation."

"Mr. Jensen, you mean we cannot enforce the probation order, if a Canadian court makes an order, because the crime is done outside of Canada?"

The defence is tongue-tied; he shrugs his shoulders.

"Your Lordship, it's impossible to do that."

I note on my pad, *We'll see about that!*

Crown counsel Roberts stands up and addresses the judge.

"Your Lordship, there is nothing in the breach of probation provision in the *Criminal Code* that makes the location of the breaching net the determinative factor for jurisdictional purpose. The appellant relies on Section 733.1(2) to argue that the location of breaching an act is the place where territorial jurisdiction for the offence of breach of probation resides. This miscasts the nature of this provision. Since in this case, Your Lordship, the provision extends jurisdiction to the place where the offender is found, even where this is another province, with the consent of the Attorney General. And, nothing in this case suggests that the province where the order was made could not also prosecute."

Grecci's lawyer launches into a preposterous defence and senior Justice Doherty, as if bored of hearing the same old argument, scratches his nose, adjusts his bifocals, clears his throat, and motions the defence counsel to proceed.

"But a strong argument can be made that the influence of marijuana can promote improper actions in social circumstances. If my client perhaps had been smoking marijuana, then marijuana can be taken as the cause of my client's improper behaviour."

Everyone stares at the defence in astonishment.

"Mr. Jensen, you don't mean to tell me that you are defending your client on the basis that he was under the influence of marijuana?" Justice Rosenberg says.

"Yes, if a person is influenced negatively by marijuana," the defence replies. The courtroom buzzes with conversation and laughter.

"So if a person smokes marijuana, you mean . . . if a person smokes marijuana, he's prone to violence?"

"Not if he smokes in moderation," Jensen says.

"That's good to hear," Justice Doherty chuckles, the crowd echoes now with more giggling, chatter, and unstoppable seat shuffling.

"And there's something else, Your Lordship. Alcohol has a printed natural warning. You get an immediate result when you use the products. Not so with marijuana."

The noise level of the crowd escalates with laughter that seems to have no end.

"Mr. Grecci has already tried to appeal his conviction twice to the Ontario Court of Appeal, for reason that

Canada has no jurisdiction to prosecute him for the breach of probation for an assault he committed in Cuba on January 4, 1999. In light of the probation and the accountability of this offence, Justice Vibert A. Lampkin has ruled Raffaele Grecci guilty on November 1999 of violating his May 1997 probation order and on December 2, 1999, sentenced Mr. Grecci to nine months imprisonment."

His Lordship Doherty pauses to scrutinize some documentation that is spread out before him. Then, he continues with his dissertation.

"Mr. Grecci, the brutal assault you have committed upon Ms. Manley could be construed as an attempted murder. In light of your committing this brutal assault upon Ms. Manley in Cuba, you can be charged only for a breach of probation order in Canada. This is a travesty! If this assault had occurred on Canadian soil, you know that under Section 6(2) of the *Criminal Code*, offenders are convicted to at least ten to fourteen years in prison."

His Justice Doherty is silent. I note in my pad, *It's unfortunate that an amendment to the* Criminal Code *has not occurred! I wish The Minister of Justice had sat through these long trials. Perhaps, the arguments and debates would have clarified my ongoing tribulations!*

His Lordship Doherty, now staring straight at Grecci, who shows no emotion, gives his conclusion,

"Mr. Justices Rosenberg, Moldaver, and I reserve decision to a later date on whether we uphold Mr. Justice Lampkin's ruling of November 22, 1999, convicting you for breaching your probation order and the December 2, 1999, sentencing of nine months in prison."

We exit the courtroom through the revolving door. Strong says,

"We were lucky that he was still on the probation order. Otherwise, there would be no trial, at all."

"Hopefully, being charge on his probation order will stop him from committing further crimes."

The journalists swarm around us. A CITY-TV crime reporter stretches out a mike.

"Are you disappointed that the justices did not reach a conclusion today?"

"Yes. It's been a long road for me. I hope that the Supreme Court will rule against Grecci's appeal, soon. In the big picture, I plan to appeal again to the Minister of Justice, asking for an amendment of a law. Not only so that other crimes of this nature will not go unpunished, but so that potential victimization might be prevented before it happens."

Detective Strong opens the car door and installs me in the seat. I lay my head against the passenger window. He speaks no more of today's events.

Chapter 23. The Final Ruling

Summer brings family activities and freedom from thoughts of my assailant. I return to oil painting and relaxing with friends. But in the back of my mind, one more court appearance awaits me. I dread having to go through it, especially seeing him in court, again.

Creativity and music lend themselves to my art, but the turmoil of preparing for yet another court date confronts me daily. I'm reminded of the injustices of the justice system. The crime lingers unresolved.

My civil lawyer and I are busy compiling, once again, the documentation on my salary slips, sick leave, and, more critical, the crime's evidence, which I have tried to forget, now. I pull out the plastic bag containing a chunk of my torn hair. It was found after the attack in the Cuban resort room.

I push thoughts of post-trauma out of my mind and focus on the small compensation. This bit is supposed to cover my pain, suffering, and the loss of work time and wages. With each sunrise, I wish it would be over—the day of the civil court.

Anna Marie, who cared for me in Cuba, arrives from Windsor a few days before the day of the civil court. In our conversations, she confirms what other witnesses have already relayed to me.

"Marisha," she says, "I believe that there's a greater purpose as to why this crime occurred to you. Yes, it's a fact that Grecci is a violent man, but he chose the wrong person to attack. Your persistence for justice will not be unheard. Marisha, how long did it take Jane Doe to advocate her case before the Canadian legal justice system before they justly provided her with a 'John Doe law' against stalking?"

In the early morning of September 11, 2001, Anna Marie, Katrina, Dan, and I head downtown to the Superior Court of Justice of Canada, located at 393 University Avenue. Before 10 A.M., we hurry into the courthouse and shuffle through the crowd to the elevators, to the eleventh floor. Sheldon, my civil lawyer, is already engaged in a conversation with the entourage of the other witnesses, Cathy and the Joyces.
   "Justice Coo is on the bench today, and we can count on a speedy trial," Sheldon announces.
   The court session is again another drawn-out revisit of my attack. More painful testimonies from the witnesses! I relive the pain, fright, and anger. I'm very surprised that I get through my own testimony without breaking down, this time. I dig my nails into my skirt as Judge Coo announces,
   "I find the accused guilty of the assault. I award compensatory damages for the total amount of $48,000, with yearly interest. The first payment is to begin on October 1."
   "At least, this blow to his pocketbook will make him think twice about assaulting anyone else!" Anna Marie says.

But what a pale victory! The amount awarded barely pays for my loss of wages, legal expenses, and other incurred expense, let alone compensate for the mental anguish and physical injuries.

A month later seems like eternity. But at last, on October 25, 2001, the Crown counsel, Gillian Roberts, excitingly informs me that Justices Doherty, Moldaver, and Rosenberg unanimously dismissed Grecci's appeal. Immediately, I log into my computer and Google search:

http://www.ontariocourts.on.ca/decisions/search/en/Ontario CourtsSearch_VOpenFile.cfm?serverFilePath=D:\Users\On tario%20Courts\www\decisions\2001\october\grecoC35784 .htm

The Judges in the thirteen-page court decision, conclude:

[45]   The appellant was bound by the terms and conditions of his May7, 1997, probation order when he violently assaulted Ms. Manley in Cuba. This assault amounted to breach of the term requiring him to keep and be of good behavior. Accordingly, I dismiss the appellant's appeal from conviction.

Signed: "M.J. MOLDAVER J.A."
"I AGREE DOHERTY J.A."
"I AGREE MARC ROSENBERG J.A."

No doubt, this ruling is just a step in the right legal direction. Grecci commences his jail sentence. Finally, the court traumas are over, and now I can breathe a few sighs of relief.

In reality, the pluses of this ruling bestow only a small consolation for the brutal crime committed against me. And I can clap all I want, but I have to live with the irony of Grecci's incarceration when my civil lawyer announces,

"Until Grecci is out of jail and gainfully employed, there will be no compensation payments awarded to you by the civil court."

All that this good news brings me is nothing but more confusion.

"Will any justice come my way?" I ask.

Then, in a few days, there's even more chaos; Grecci's lawyer launches yet another appeal, this time to the Supreme Court of Canada.

His defense posts bail; his jail term is cut short and Grecci is free again. On top of that, while Grecci is out on bail, he personally calls and alerts my civil lawyer to relay to me that he's unable to make his damage payments to me.

"The system keeps failing me!" I tell everyone.

"The precedent-setting means nothing to me. Grecci is testing the law's deficiency. Because the real point of the law is overlooked, I am victimized by the justice system!"

Everyone I meet patiently listens.

"My assailant forces his appeals to have the conviction overturned. His lawyer enters a brief for acquittal, based on two reasons. First, he argues that Grecci was not required to comply with the terms and conditions of his probation order while outside Canada. And second, he argues that even if he was required to comply with the probation order, while out of Canada, s. 5(2) of the

Criminal Code "prevents" him from being convicted, because the offence was committed in Cuba, not Canada," I keep repeating.

"I hope you find peace somehow," they respond.
"I hope the Minister of Justice will reply positively this time to my appeal to her condescending first response. Perhaps the Minister of Justice will live up to the title and take action with the deserved justice!"

Fall turns to winter, all is in a frozen state, and so is the response from the Minister of Justice. There's nothing anyone can do or say. Even my psychologist can only offer this encouragement,
"Marisha, you have handled this case so far; you can see it thought the end. Stay focused and strong!"

A long, brisk winter passes; the tiny heads of crocuses now peek through, giving hope for a new life. I seek the outside sun, taking many walks, as I wait for some kind of just resolution. On April 18, 2002, Detective Strong calls, and with excitement announces,

"The Ontario Court of Appeal upholds Justice Lampkin's decision. The judgment reads, *Application for leave to appeal from the judgment of the Court of Appeal for Ontario, Number C35784, dated October 25, 2001, was this day dismissed!"*
Finally, the Court of Appeal released reasons, dismissing the appeal. They are reported at (2001), 159 C.C.C. (3d) 146 (Ont.C.A.).

Grecci is sentenced to a paltry nine-month jail term with a three-year probation order, plus a ten-year restraining order preventing him from coming anywhere near me.

"Well, at least the Supreme Court of Canada did not allow Grecci to get away with the breach of his probation!" Everyone knows that this crime has never been vindicated. The assailant has slipped through the legal system without a charge! Grecci got away without indictment for his crime against me in Cuba.

All who have become aware of the inadequacy of the *Canadian Criminal Code* 6(2) keep asking,

"When will the Canadian legal justice system justly respond with a jurisdictional law in the *Canadian Criminal Code* so that the shocking crimes committed abroad by a Canadian upon another Canadian will be charged by the Canadian justice system?"

Epilogue

As I explore my ordeal, not as a subject, but as a writer, I also am resolute to perform a delicate balance. The last thing I would expect is to come across as a victim. Neither do I desire to negate and forget the support of everyone who has encouraged along the way. Especially, I do not want to dismiss those who have implored me to tell my story.

Sometimes my mind drifts, and I ponder the wisdom of my decision.

I could just put the pen down and let others contend with the "complicated" legal cases. But would that be the just thing to do when the news broadcasts similar chronic crimes, which cannot be charged in Canada?

With my understanding of all that I suffered and learned, could I live with myself by remaining still and letting others deal with the unresolved justice? Or should I hand in my bag of documentation and newspaper clippings to someone else?

Then I wake up, as if from a bad dream, and ask: Who else could chronicle my narrative with the necessary intensity and passion? My resolution is not to remain silent and bury the truth about the inadequacy of the *Canadian Criminal Code*. Otherwise I would neglect my responsibility as a free and a proud Canadian.

I find no sense that my democratic country Canada embraces a legal system that doesn't care about justice for the common citizen.

Take it from me! If you travel extensively, I suggest that you find out how much your government will do to protect your Canadian human rights in specific sovereign countries.

It is one thing to be a soldier protected by rules established by the Geneva Convention and enforced by international law, but what protection is available to the average Canadian traveling abroad?

An enormous number of Canadians who travel throughout the world believe that their rights are solidly protected, and all they need to do is run to their nearest consulate or embassy. My story graphically illustrates that glaring insufficiencies and ambiguities exist in the current Canadian federal statutes.

When another Canadian assaulted me while I traveled abroad, I became not only a victim of that brutal crime, but also a casualty of obtrusive, outdated Canadian laws. For years I found myself struggling to find protection from my Canadian attacker, and a ruling for that crime within these blatant miscarriages of the Canadian legal system.

Canadians, like myself, are setting the wheels in motion to amend a jurisdictional law for the Canadian justice system to grant their citizens a jurisdictional protection that extends beyond "diplomats, victims of aircraft hijacking, hostage taking, protection of nuclear materials, torture, war crimes, piracy" to the entire Canadian population.

As a reader, if you agree with my conclusions, would you kindly write to:

Office of the Prime Minister
80 Wellington Street
Ottawa, ON K1A 0A2

The Minister of Justice and Attorney General of Canada
284 Wellington St
Ottawa, ON K1A 0H8

Please state that Canada should allow the prosecution of Canadians in Canada for crimes committed in foreign places that are already part of the Canadian Criminal Code. While it may not necessarily create a change overnight, however your voice will be part of the water on stone that is needed to erode the existing indifference.
Moreover, it would be appreciated if you could post your letter in the Guest Book on the website:
www.holidayinhell.ca

Thank you

Send me ___ copies of *Holiday in Hell*.

Add postage and handling for a single book: $8.00 CAD in Canada, $10.00 International.
For more copies in the same order please dd $2.00 CAD each.
Book price: $19.95 CAD Total for books:_____ CAD. Total handling charges: _____ CAD
　　　　Grand total: _____ CAD

Full Name: _____
Company: _____
Shipping Address: _____
City: _____ State: _____
Country: _____ Zip/Postal Code: _____
☐ Money order enclosed
Charge my ☐ VISA ☐ MC Account #: ☐☐☐☐☐☐☐☐☐☐☐☐ Expiry: ☐☐/☐☐
Signature: _____

ASTEROID
PUBLISHINGinc

Please make your cheques payable to:
Asteroid Publishing Inc.,,
P.O. Box 3, Richmond Hill, ON Canada
L4C 4X9

Quantity dsicounts: 25% for 5 or more.